A Small Corner of ⌐⌐⌐

John Holland, Pat Hooper, Martin Howard

redcliffe

In memory of Dorothy Pike
1911– 2007

and John Hickery
1942–2009

I was born on the sixth of January 1911. Came with the camels
– the feast of Epiphany is the sixth of January. My children used to say,
'Mother, you came with the camels, you always had the hump!'

Dorothy Pike

First published in 2009 by Redcliffe Press Ltd.,
81g Pembroke Road, Bristol BS8 3EA

www.redcliffepress.co.uk
info@redcliffepress.co.uk

© John Holland, Pat Hooper, Martin Howard
All drawings © Anton Bantock

ISBN 978-1-906593-41-4

British Library Cataloguing-in-Publication Data
A catalogue record for this book is available from the British Library

Design and typesetting by Crescent Creative, www.crescentcreative.co.uk
Printed by HSW Print, Tonypandy, Rhondda

CONTENTS

ACKNOWLEDGEMENTS

The editors would like to thank the following people and organisations for their help, support and encouragement in producing this book:

Anton Bantock for his original drawings of the Ashton Gate area; everyone who contributed photographs; Quartet Community Foundation for a Grassroots Grant to enable production and publication; Available Light Productions Limited for a donation towards design costs; Bristol City Council Record Office and, above all, the people who shared their life stories without which the book would not exist.

INTRODUCTION

This book celebrates the lives of twenty five people who all have one thing in common: that they have lived in the Ashton Gate area of Bristol for many years. Their life stories are typical of people of their particular generations, born in the first half of the twentieth century. The setting is a small triangle of roads in BS3 – bounded by Walter Street and Coronation Road to the east, Frayne Road to the south west, with Clift House Road to the north and Clift Road running through the middle. This 'small corner' of Bristol which provides the backdrop against which the stories are set is, perhaps, also typical of its type: a cluster of streets lined by terraced houses which were built in the early years of the twentieth century. Other prominent features of the area are Greville Smyth Park, the Clift House Road Tannery, and the southernmost of three vast, red-brick warehouses, built as bonded storage for Bristol's one-time tobacco industry.

The book describes how the local community has changed over the years, as local employment opportunities have waxed and waned and shops have appeared, changed hands and, in many cases, been lost for good. However, in spite of the changes, the sense of neighbourliness and pride at being part of this community are recurrent themes.

The idea of producing the book grew out of celebrations, organised by a local community group, to mark the centenary of the construction of the houses in this part of Bristol. A letter published in the *Bristol Evening Post* outlined our plans and asked people with an interest in sharing their life stories to make contact with members of the small project team overseeing the work. As a result of this and a further article in a community magazine serving the area, a number of people got in touch and were subsequently interviewed. Many, but not all, were elderly and in some cases have lived in this part of the city for all of their lives. Their stories provide rich details of everyday life.

With full permission from all those interviewed, their stories were recorded and subsequently transcribed, the aim being to add to existing archives, such as the Bristol City Council Record Office. Once the wealth of material which we gleaned had been analysed, several major themes – such as family life, local shops and life during the war – emerged. Wherever possible, we have used the actual words of those interviewed, interspersed by short sections of narrative which serve to set the scene, as well as linking and contextualising the stories, and also highlighting items of particular interest.

Like most books which are based on people's memories, a few inaccuracies are bound to occur. In addition, familiar places are often referred to by a variety of names – such as Greville Smyth Park, known locally as Ashton Park. We also know that shops changed owners, and names, as the years went by and we apologise in advance if any mistakes in the book cause offence to readers. Throughout the book, people are referred to by their current name, married rather than maiden names being used where applicable. A list of all those who contributed their stories is included and maiden names given there.

The project has provided an opportunity for people to reflect on their lives. It has enabled them to recall events, and by giving them a 'voice', it will ensure that their memories are recorded so that these can be shared and passed on. The sense of ownership and pride in what has been achieved by all concerned is very tangible.

John Holland
Pat Hooper
Martin Howard

Ashton Gate 2009

WHO IS WHO IN THE BOOK

A Small Corner of Bristol is based on the life stories of the following people. Maiden names arc given in brackets. The name of the road where each person lived, or still lives, in the Ashton Gate area is provided by way of context.

Eddie Beaven	Clift Road
Alma Chalmers (Payne)	Walter Street
Mary Butt (Hall)	Clift Road
Bernard Chalmers	Gerald Road
Hazel Coles (Williams)	Ashton Road, Coronation Road
Jantzen Derrick	Ashton Road, Frayne Road, Clift Road
Tony Gingell	Frayne Road
Sheila Hall (Rowe)	Coronation Road
Brenda Hatter (Baylis)	Coronation Road
Len Hatter	Raynes Road, Clift Road
Barbara Hickery (Nolder)	Clift Road
John Hickery	Clift Road
Lewis ('Lew') Pedler	Clift Road
Dorothy Pike (Collins)	Ashton Gate Terrace, Clift Road
Pam Reed (Smith)	Frayne Road
	(previously, Sandy Park Road, Brislington)
Roland Reed	Frayne Road
David Ridley	Clift House Road
Thelma Short (Short)	Clift House Road, Clift Road
Mervyn Southway	Clift House Road
Janet Steel (Amesbury)	Frayne Road
Karen Thomas (Gingell)	Frayne Road
Peggy Triggle	Clift Road
Sheila Williamson (Triggle)	Clift Road
Stephen Williamson	Clift Road
Kath Winter (O'Farrell)	Frayne Road

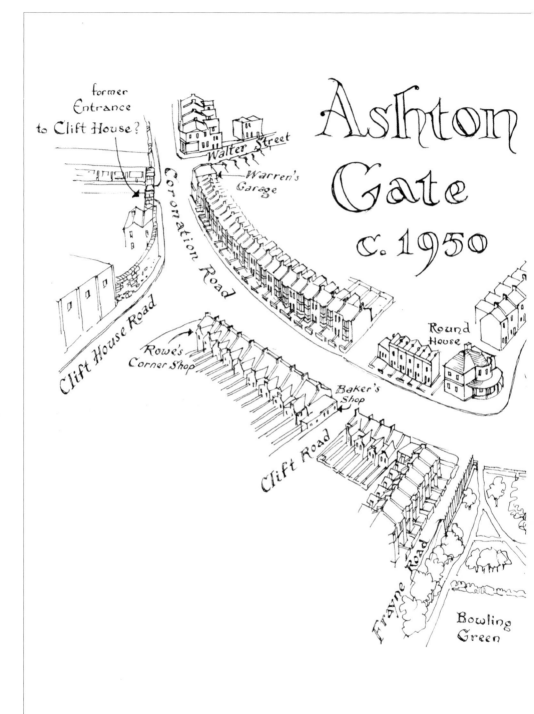

former
Entrance
to Clift House?

Walter Street

Warren's Garage

Ashton Gate
c. 1950

Coronation Road

Clift House Road

Rowe's Corner Shop

Round House

Baker's Shop

Clift Road

Fryne Road

Bowling Green

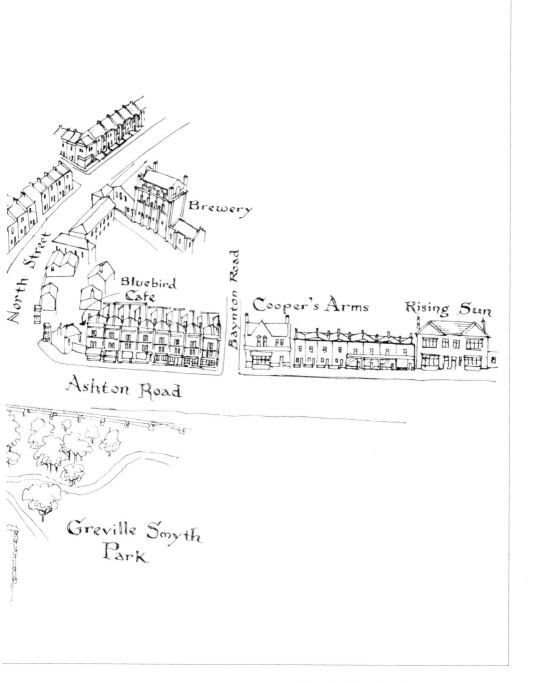

Brewery

North Street

Baynton Road

Bluebird Cafe

Cooper's Arms

Rising Sun

Ashton Road

Greville Smyth Park

Chapter 1

FAMILIES, FRIENDS AND NEIGHBOURS

My mum, she used to go out the front, she used to sweep in front of the house, she'd call it her barton. I don't know what they call it really, but it was a little square, and she'd brush the front, she'd brush the pavement.

Hazel Coles

Many people reading this book will be familiar with the Ashton Gate area – perhaps growing up or raising a family here, or maybe having recently moved into one of the houses. In this chapter, people who know this part of Bristol well describe what it has been like for them to have lived here for a number of years. Their stories describe everyday family life, close friends and other people who lived nearby.

What brought people to this part of the city? Karen Thomas's family moved here to be close to relatives:

My mother's sister and her husband [were] the Wyatts. They had the Rising Sun pub opposite the park and my parents moved out this way because they liked the area and mum wanted to be near her sister so she could help out in the pub when they were needed, so that's how that came about.

David Ridley was born and brought up in Exeter Road and then moved into one of the distinctive semi-detached properties on Clift House Road which are owned by the tannery:

My grandfather owned a farm out at Cleeve in the 1900s and he came into Bristol to open up the Thomas Ware & Sons tannery with Mr Brierley who bought it and he came in and sold his little farm business and then of course me grandfather worked there. Our dad, when he was foreman, his house, you know where the factory is and next door there's two houses set back, looks like Dutch houses. Well we lived in one of them, the end one, nearest to the garden centre and when we went in there it was beautiful. They were owned by the tannery. But of course when me dad was taken ill and he had to pack work up we had to leave.

Roland and Pam Reed had been seeking a house in Frayne Road for some time:

Well, my mother was an elderly persons' concert troupe singer although she was 70ish herself. She entertained the elderly, and a friend of hers who lived in Ashton Road said there was a property in Frayne Road and that was 1960 or '61. We moved here in October 1961. There was an elderly lady who had just died. Maurice, her son, lived in Long Ashton and it was up for sale. We made an offer and unfortunately we couldn't get a mortgage as you can nowadays, which seems so silly because we had a fair deposit. One of our guarantors was Jessie Stephens. She was very strong in the Labour movement.

Like many whose life stories are told in this book, Lew Pedler was born and brought up in the area, living in a house in Clift Road which his grandfather had bought in 1907 for £200:

I was born on the 17th October 1942 and lived at 21 Clift Road because that was the home of my parents who had lived there for two years as a married couple, but my grandfather actually owned the house so my mother and father went to live there after they got married. It's interesting that although I lived there until 1964 until I got married and obviously my parents continued to live there, so I still had touch with the area until my father died in 1982. The house was sold in 1983.

Having lived in Bower Ashton for a time, Dorothy Pike's mother moved to Ashton Gate Terrace where Dorothy was born in 1911, later moving to Clift Road where Dorothy lived for the rest of her life and brought up three sons:

> That was my home. I've lived here all my life. Yes, all my 96 years. First at Ashton Gate Terrace and then here. I did go to Upton Road for a little while, but I was very unhappy there. I didn't get on with my in-laws at all. So then we moved in here. And I've been very, very happy here, very happy indeed.

The Derrick family moved from nearby Pearl Street just after the war ended and Jantzen can clearly recall several events from his early childhood, including details of the move itself:

> We moved to Ashton Road, which I think was number 7, opposite the park gates at this end, the 'round house' end of Ashton Road. We moved in there in about 1945 or '46. The big, tall houses between the Red and White Café as it is now and

Looking along Ashton Road, Greville Smyth Park on the right, with its original railings. The short parade of shops on the left, mentioned frequently in the book, is now converted into private houses, with just the Red and White café remaining. Note the overhead tram wires. (Courtesy of Memories Photos, Bristol)

Some of the Williams family and their friends in the back garden of 247 Coronation Road. Behind is Hazel Williams holding Georgina. Middle row left to right: Pat Bush, Molly Williams, Brenda Hatter. Front row left to right: Roger, Maureen.

Brenda Hatter in her back garden, 241 Coronation Road, taken in 1949. The flowers on the mound behind Brenda cover the roof of a wartime Anderson shelter.

Brenda Hatter aged about 3 in 1938 at her parents' allotment. The allotment was situated on the site of the current Riverside Garden Centre, behind C Bond warehouse in Clift House Road.

Another photo showing Brenda on her parents' allotment, this one taken in 1937.

the empty shop at the far end. There's about four or five houses there. And then we moved from there across the road into number 2 Frayne Road, and I say, apart from the fact that mum and dad didn't want to spend money on removals, it was a bit ridiculous having a removal van anyway! So we just trundled across the road carrying all the furniture and bits and pieces really, into Frayne Road. I was there for probably about ten years I should think. We lived there, we shared the house with my mum's sister and she lived in the front part of the house and we lived in the back. They're both gone now, my uncle and my auntie. My auntie Doreen it was, they never had any children. We lived there till I was 15 and we parted company then and moved over to Bedminster Road in Bedminster. I was about 15. My earliest memory is my gran sending me down to buy certain things – which was like a gas mantle because the house was lit by gas. She'd send me down to get a gas mantle, three cigarettes, half a pound of butter – small things like that.

Mervyn Southway was renting rooms in 3 Clift House Road in the early 1950s when the landlord and his wife died soon after one another and the opportunity to purchase the whole house arose:

Well they had to sell the properties – and there was quite a few properties he had – so they approached us and said were we interested, you see. So they said, make an offer. Of course I had a word with a friend of mine who worked for some building society. So we decided to offer £500 – in fact they accepted £640. So we bought it for £640 on mortgage. So, you know, we told them we didn't have any money – people didn't have any money in those days – so there was no way we could put down a deposit or do anything of the sort, so they were quite prepared to overlook that. They even arranged the mortgage for us with Bradford and Bingley! So from there on, we took it over 15 years because of the age of the house it had to be 15 years – they would do 20 years for those houses built then. I think the mortgage we paid was one pound eight shillings per week, but even then it wasn't easy when you consider that the wage was about £6 a week.

Until she moved to Nailsea in 2007, Mary Butt's house – 1 Clift Road – had been owned by her late husband's family for three generations, as she explains:

Mr and Mrs Knowles [my grandparents] moved in about 1920. He had two grocery shops in Hotwells and serviced the Campbell's steamers up to the Second World War. My mother-in-law, Mrs Dorothy Butt, moved from 24 Clift Road to her parents' house in 1924 with her three children, Doreen, Vernon and Lionel. She had married John Butt, the eldest son of Walter Butt, who owned seven grocery shops, known as Butts Stores, the registered shop being 7 North Street. In 1950, Lionel and I set up home there [1 Clift Road] on a temporary basis! In the coming years we had three children, Sylvia, David and Philip. Unfortunately my husband died in 2002 and after five years, I decided I needed to move into something smaller and so moved to be nearer my sons.

Another family which had lived in the area since the houses were built in the early years of the twentieth century were the Shorts:

My grandparents lived in the end house – nearest the park – of Clift House Road. At the side of the house was a lane at the back of the houses in Clift Road. This would be about 1900. My father lived there with his brothers and sisters. It was a grand house, double-fronted with a balcony. My parents married and emigrated to Australia where they lived for ten years before coming back to England. Before they left, a photo was taken [see p152] of the whole family standing on the balcony. (Thelma Short)

Thelma met and later married a man with the same surname as hers and they went to live in two rooms at his parents' house, 2 Clift Road:

The road seemed to be full of relations of my new husband! His grandma lived opposite and then there were two aunts and uncles.

Because of their generous sizes, the houses in the streets which form the 'Ashton Gate triangle' have traditionally been occupied by families. At one time it was common practice for children to continue to live in their parents' house, even after they had married and perhaps had children of their own. Stephen Williamson remembers what it was like being the youngest of three generations living in a four-bedroomed house:

Grandfather and grandmother lived there, mum, mum's sister, dad and myself. Yes, we were just at the stage of it becoming overcrowded because at the age of seven, I was still sleeping in the same bedroom with mum and dad and we'd certainly been looking at houses up in the Hengrove area. Then grandfather died which sort of created mum's sister to go in with her mother in the big front bedroom and I was given the little bedroom and mum and dad had the back bedroom and that's how it continued until, well it stayed that way while I was at college until I got married and then things changed round.

Kath Winter also recalls the tight squeeze of family life, made easier when one of her daughters married and moved out:

Five children – yes – and Pop. Well we had four bedrooms. I had four girls but one boy. Gary had the little bedroom, Pop had the bedroom at the back, we had the middle bedroom and the girls had the big bedroom. I don't s'pose we were down that many years when Tina got married.

What was the Ashton Gate area like in the period immediately before and after the last war? Several people remember it as being quite an affluent corner of Bristol, attracting people with a professional occupation and those running their own businesses:

It was very refined. I wouldn't say we were wealthy, but what I would call comfortable – well-dressed. (Peggy Triggle)

In fact we had our clothes tailored, the clothes that my mother didn't make – dresses and things, skirts and kilts. We always had to wear kilts and they were always tailored. But we weren't wealthy, we were fortunate. We didn't think so at the time, but we realise now, that my grandfather decided that the house was big enough for all four to live in – so we did, my mother suffering from ill-health quite a lot it was handy, except that my grandmother was a bit of a martinet. We had to behave ourselves. (Sheila Williamson)

Mr and Mrs William and Susannah Baylis and their children taken approx 1909 at Tannery Cottage, Coronation Road. Pictured left to right: Rear: William, George (Brenda Hatter's father), Catherine, Elizabeth, Susannah (née Harris). Front: William, Frederick.

Sheila Hall's aunt, Eliza Smith, with their cat Champ, in 1956. They are seated outside Tommy Rowe's corner shop at 300 Coronation Road, at the junction with Clift House Road. The shop was demolished for road alterations in the 1960s. The land just behind Eliza was where Tommy Rowe displayed various goods, and the brick building behind this was his storage space. The poster pasted on the wall is for the Blagdon Show.

Sheila Hall, her father Tommy Rowe and their cat Champ. The picture was taken near their shop, with a solitary Morris Minor progressing along Clift House Road.

Sheila Hall and her father Tommy Rowe outside his shop, in April 1958. Sheila recalls that the shop was entered through double-doors at an angle on the corner of Coronation Road and Clift House Road. Tommy was never without his cap!

Sisters Margaret Triggle and Sheila Williamson with friends and relatives in the garden of 32 Clift Road. The picture was taken around 1938-9, the event possibly being a birthday. Relatives include their Aunt Kath Simpson and cousins John and Alan, also of Clift Road.

Lew Pedler has a clear idea of the neighbourhood gained from meeting people on a regular basis when, as a boy, he did a milk round in the area:

I think a lot of people that lived in Clift Road on the basis of ownership were either tradesmen or they were salesmen, both of which could be considered to be jobs that had a reasonable income. So far as Frayne Road was concerned I think you'll find the higher social classes were there, probably the managers or owners of small businesses or offspring of. That was the picture I got from a very early age.

Janet Steel, born and brought up in Frayne Road, recalls it as being 'quite a refined road.' Mervyn Southway remembers visiting 'that big house' on the corner of Frayne Road [number 1] which was where Charlie Stenner lived at the time:

I went in there many times and in there they still had the bells from years ago when they had a maid. You had a box with all these different rooms on, and whichever room it was, the bell would ring and the maid would go – not in my auntie's time

— long before that. But they still had it in the house. They've probably had it taken down now, I imagine. And of course he also owned a garage for a car and my uncle sold it to Len Sutton.

Not being able to afford a car, Roland and Pam Reed bought a motorbike and sidecar which they had to park in the street, little realising how some of the neighbours would react:

It wasn't the thing in Frayne Road! My mother always said 'Frayne Road is a nice road.' She always wanted us not to miss that opportunity. I always remember going to the Post Office with my tax disc for the bike on a Saturday morning and when I came back the police were there because there was no tax disc and I'm sure that was done by neighbours.

Mary Butt recalls the area in the 1950s:

No cars. Quite a number of professionals — teachers, that sort of person. Quite a sedate road [Clift Road]. Before the war, the area was referred to as 'Ashton Park'. Grandma's calling card had Ashton Park on it, not 'Gate'.

Family life

What was family life like fifty or sixty years ago? Hazel Coles was one of six children when her parents moved into the end house on Ashton Road, near the main entrance to Bristol City Football Club, in the early years of the war:

There was a shop on the front which wasn't open and we had a big house like, behind the shop. Well, my younger sister was born there, in the bedroom above the shop. I think she was born in about 1942. Then we moved from Ashton Road to Coronation Road, 247 Coronation Road, and we went there when my sister was about I should think she was two or not quite two and then we 'ad our friends round there.

Hazel has fond memories of her mother and the hard work she did to bring up her family:

She was a good mother. She was always home, waiting for the children to come home and cooking and cleaning. She was a wonderful mother, but very strict. I mean we were never allowed out late, we always had to be in, 'cos in them days no televisions but we used to listen to the wireless and every night at a certain time, Dick Barton Special Agent used to come on, and we'd all sit up and listen. And then after that finished, she made us like – the boys had to do different things and learn, you know, perhaps they done a bit of painting or something and I was the eldest girl, and she used to teach me to knit and I used to have to knit my gloves for the winter and of course we had to darn our socks you know, and she taught me how to darn. We were all busy, always doing something.

Being the eldest child of a large family meant extra responsibilities for Hazel:

We managed, you know. I used to cook, because my mother brought us up like, to cook. My youngest brother, he used to come running home from school, dinner time, 'cos we always had to go home for dinner, and run back to school again and he'd help. He'd be doing the toast, I'd be doing the eggs, then he ran back to school and this is how we went on and they always had a cooked tea. Then about 6 o'clock, mum would be coming home and I used to put the two babies in the pram, the baby one up the top and the other down the bottom and push the pram through Ashton Park to meet her. And the other ones, they used to be on the swings over Ashton Park they used to run on in front of us.

In contrast to the Williams family, the Butts in Clift Road were wealthy enough to afford to employ a maid:

The last maid was a young girl from South Wales. When the war was declared, her mother came and took her away.

Hazel Coles also remembers only too well how fragile family life became when serious illness occurred:

My dad was taken ill and he was taken to Southmead Hospital for 12 months. So I was the big sister, and my little sister was a month old when he went into hospital and I'd just had an operation on my leg, so I couldn't go to school because I was in Plaster-of-Paris. And my other little sister, Maureen, was two and Georgina was a month old, and plus we had two brothers and another sister. There were six of us and my dad was, well, they didn't know whether he had TB or pleurisy and they gave mum a white card [or] white letter to say he was dangerously ill and wasn't expected to live. Course there was no telephones like, you know, not in those days and they sent the police a couple of times for mum to go. So she used to get up in the morning and get ready and go off out to Southmead Hospital and she used to have to walk through Ashton Park, down to Hotwells to get the bus, get to Southmead, and I was left home. I suppose I was about 13, I think I was and I had to look after the family and the baby – she was only a month old. I used to bath her, dress her, feed her, see to her, then the other one that was two. But the funny part about it, the one that was two she sort of wanted to make a fuss of the baby, so what my mother done, she had a wicker clothes basket and she padded it and lined it and we used to put the baby in there and put her on top of the table back by the wall so the one that was two couldn't grab her. Well dad was away for 12 months and then eventually he came home, but I just had to look after the family. Because we never had anybody to look after us and of course it's not like today, you know, when there was help or anything.

Other people also have memories of injuries, trips to hospital and the impact on family life:

I can remember it was in the winter of 1946–47 so it was icy and that's about the first distinctive memory I have although around about that time I can remember my father coming home in an ambulance round about Christmas time because he'd been gassed because he was a plumber with the docks and he was working in a confined space in Cumberland Basin and I suspect he was in there smoking his pipe and having a little nice quiet time and the gas was turned on filled up the space and he was dragged out. He was taken away to hospital and a few days later was carted home. I think I spent quite an enjoyable Christmas because he was home. I can also remember a train set which I set up quite happily and he was there to add the bits and pieces. (Lew Pedler)

Clift Road. Terraced houses built c1910, although nos. 13–17 were destroyed by bombs during the war and subsequently rebuilt. One of the pair of cottages owned by the Tannery can be seen in the distance, as well as the top of C Bond warehouse.

3 Clift House Road, looking towards Ashton Court which can be seen in the distance. The southernmost of three vast, red brick 'bonded warehouses' dominates the road at this point.

As a boy, Eddie Beavan spent most school holidays staying with his uncle and aunt in Clift Road. They kept a shop and, having no children of their own, treated Eddie like a son:

> Yes it was a nice time, a nice childhood you know. When he [Eddie's uncle, Edwin Stubbs] had time off – I suppose in those days, like they do today, shut the shop on a Wednesday afternoon – I remember him taking me up the cinema on North Street, on the corner of Raleigh Road, the Plaza. We went up there like and there was a little newsagents where the roundhouse is, on the corner and he always got his cigarettes there and comics. He'd buy loads of comics. He liked *The Beano*, *The Dandy*, I think it was *The Topper* – about half a dozen different comics. And he'd come home and he'd read them as well. And the cigarettes he used to buy was Turf and on the back of the packet was a little photograph of different breeds of dog and he used to cut all those out – well save the packets like. Other packets he used to let me have because in those days you could play cigarette packets in the road 'cos there wasn't no traffic then. You'd sit on the kerb and flick the cigarette packets against the wall and whoever you played against like, if your cigarette packet went on top of theirs, you'd win the pile like. Funny things! It passed the time. Brooke Bond tea I believe they used to have and he used to save the little cards. They did cards in there of animals and different things; he'd save all them. You used to call them 'generals' at one time, years ago. I think they're worth quite a bit of money now they are. I used to save all those. I used to have a box of them at one time, all bound up like. I don't know what happened to those actually. Yeah, I can remember him saving me these little ones with Turf, with the dogs on. The little things that you remember.

Small but significant events feature large in people's memories:

> In 1958 we had a refrigerator! I can remember it coming. I had a stream of endless ice lollies. I was given a little plastic mould in the shape of a rabbit and by mixing up orange squash and freezing it you had ice lollies. Oh yes, I remember it well. It was just this dream of ice lollies, I think. Gosh, you had something in the house that would always provide you with an ice lolly! I remember being in Ashton Gate on the afternoon of it being delivered and very anxious to get home and then

Cousins Miles Wyatt and Karen Thomas, August 1961. Miles's mum and dad, Kitty and Fred, were running the Rising Sun public house, opposite the park in Ashton Road.

Karen Thomas outside her home at 32 Frayne Road, sporting a wig and clothes she had brought home from a working trip to the USA.

Karen Thomas with her Jack Russell, Boo, standing by the beech tree in Greville Smyth Park in 1967.

Terry Maloney, who lived at 7 Frayne Road, and Karen Thomas, taken outside Karen's house at 32 Frayne Road in 1962.

of course very, very impatient because they don't freeze in seconds. It was quite disappointing having to wait so long and it wasn't exactly the best ice lolly I've ever tasted but I was making them myself. (Stephen Williamson)

In the days when a television set was an expensive luxury and long before home computers were invented, children had to seek their own amusements, as Karen Thomas recalls:

We had a dog [called Boo] and I used to go for very long walks. I used to walk along the tow path up through Leigh Woods, across the Suspension Bridge and down or I used to just take the dog up Rownham Hill and round, I used to go miles I used to walk and walk with the dog. In fact we used to have a duck. My mother used to love ducks and she had an Aylesbury duck and I was ill one time and the chap who owned the place the hairdressing salon in Brook Street – Joanne's – came round and was in the front room and the duck walked in straight across in front of him and sat in the fireplace and he didn't bat an eyelid. He didn't say what's that duck doing, he just ignored the whole thing. It was hilarious! Mother also rescued a magpie and took it to the vet and was feeding it pills because it kept falling over. She kept it in the middle room, where we had the piano, and of course the thing kept messing all over the place. She nursed it back to health and then got fed up with it and purposely left the door open so it left of its own accord.

Karen describes the fun she had as a teenager, perhaps typical for young people in the 1950s and '60s:

We didn't go into town, no. I always had a boyfriend and either you'd go and sit in someone's front room of one or other's parents. Terry [Karen's brother] and Tim, who actually became my husband, had motorbikes and then they graduated to cars. Other friends of Tim's used to borrow their fathers' cars to go out and we used to go to places like Portishead or Clevedon and we used to have a portable radio in the back blaring. There was a time on a weekend we used to get in the car, and we used to be four in the car and we used to take it in turns to be picked to go in one direction out from Bristol and we used to rate the pubs from the outside out of ten and then you'd go in and you'd rate it then what the inside was like!

Frlends and neighbours

Then, as now, having good neighbours and friends who lived nearby counted for much:

Ada Wedlock and I were very great friends. She died on my kitchen floor. Came in with a birthday card, asked Robert to drop it down somebody's, and just dropped dead on the floor. It was rather sad, we were great friends. She was a bit younger than me. Fred Wedlock was her cousin. She had three brothers. One of them has died. Clive is still alive I think. Her father was Fatty Wedlock, the footballer. She lived in the pub [the Star on Ashton Road, later renamed Wedlocks] until she got married, and then she lived up here, and eventually her father came to live up here with her, when he retired, in Clift House Road. (Dorothy Pike)

Trusted neighbours often shared the important task of looking after their friends' children:

Well we left Greville Road and went over our mum's for a bit and that's where I had my daughter down there. Stayed with mother for a while. When our daughter got a bit bigger she used to go out. I used to sit her in her pram out the front and leave her there and outside the shops. Yeah, leave her out the front and everyone used to talk to her. Then when she got a bit bigger she'd be going up the street and I didn't know whose house she'd be in. They'd say 'It's alright — she's in 'ere.' She'd be in one of the neighbours' houses. (Barbara Hickery)

Growing up during the war, Janet Steel remembers playing with other children living in her street [Frayne Road] as well as the kindness shown to her by several neighbours, including those with no children of their own:

Freda and Doris Fewsell. It's not Fussell — it's Fewsell — but I can't remember how it's written, but they were good friends of my father's and they lived at number 7. Number 6 were the Rogers family. They had two children called Gregory and Jane. I suppose he was about three or four years younger — something like that. Number 11 — that was Mrs Pont and Gwen. I never knew a Mr Pont, and that was flats, number 11. There were two families. Mrs Pont and her daughter they lived

The Gillard family of 13 Frayne Road, taken
around 1939.
Left to right:
Laurie Gillard (best man)
Stan Cook (bridegroom)
Kathleen Cook (bride) (Gillard)
Maisie Gillard (bridesmaid)

Janet Amesbury, who lived at
12 Frayne Road, in the Gillard's
back garden at 13 Frayne Road,
around 1937.

Mr and Mrs Gillard, their daughter Maisie and grand-
daughter (name unknown) in their garden at 13 Frayne
Road. Taken in the early 1940s.

downstairs, and upstairs it was Mr and Mrs Babbage, Gertie and George. She was lovely – well they both were. Number 15 were Mr and Mrs Boulton. Number 16 – Mrs Denmead. She was an elderly lady and she had a daughter Mary. Yes, I think there was a son – I don't remember. I used to call her Gran Denmead and used to spend quite a lot of time with her. She was a really sweet old lady.

Janet also remembers her special friends who lived just round the corner in Clift Road:

Mr and Mrs Harris, they had… there was Reggie – he was older than me – and there was Pat. Pat was the same, about my age and I believe there was a little one as well. But I can remember Mr Harris – he was working, I think he must have worked for the railways because on this particular day, Mrs Harris said to Pat and I, 'Will you and Pat do something for me? Will you go and take some sandwiches to your dad?' And so Pat said yes – so she said, 'I'll just do them now.' And she did fried bread sandwiches and dipped them in sugar afterwards so they were warm. And Mr Harris was working down – you had to go past the park, over the road and he was working down on the railway line where it went under the bridge – under the swing bridge.

In a time when having good manners mattered perhaps more than they do today, it was an unwritten rule that children should show respect to adults at all times. When breaches occurred, one's parents were usually informed and appropriate punishment meted out, as Lew Pedler remembers only too well!

Where we used to get trouble from parents was if people came and knocked on the door and complained so say we might have given some old buck. I can remember particularly number 6 [Clift Road] was a Miss Bryan who lived with her father and she was a pianist, a tall lady but she was quite a fierce woman and she used to be looking out of her window all the time if our ball went into her garden and you literally daren't go into her garden, she'd be out the front door and the only way you could retrieve the ball was if it had gone into the bushes and you could see it from a distance and creep along under the wall and somebody would say 'Just there' and you'd try and grab the ball back. Sometimes if she did catch you and you had run away, and she was on the knocker, if that had happened, I suppose because we'd run away from responsibility, that's when my mother, it was always my mother, my father never did, my father used to lose his temper and be lost for words and I'd burst into laughter and that was the end of it, but when mother let fly I knew I was onto it. Short trousers of course were lethal and she always used to catch you on the back of the leg. The time it stopped, she hit me so hard one day she almost brought tears to her own eyes, not because it hurt her because she left such a wheal mark at the back of my legs it gave her a conscience she said 'I'll never do that again' and I breathed a sigh of relief! I suppose I was about nine or ten then.

Undeterred, Lew and his friends continued to plague the neighbours:

Now we used to have run-ins with Mr Sage. Mr and Mrs Sage, they had an immaculate house. I think she must have been a housekeeper in her days. Early in the morning as soon as daylight arrived she would be out on her knees scrubbing the front step daily. But I knew his garden well because we used to have to get into his garden when we wanted the ball back when we were playing cricket in the lane. He had one serious problem with us particularly well with his cats. My father was passionate about making sure his tomatoes and his beans had no bugs on them so he was always able to get from somewhere these syringes. When he was out of the way or out at work, Bob [Pike] and I used to fill these syringes up with water and wait for the Sage's cat to be perched on his gatepost and give this cat a great squirt of water up his backside! Well the cat used to scarper like crazy and the spray used to go everywhere and of course the problem was that old Sage was sat in his garden. So needless to say we were caught doing it and he used to go absolutely berserk. We were terrified! We used to shoot in the back garden and put the bolt on he used to be hiding behind the wall and he'd put his fingers on the wall trying to climb over and see us.

Having assisted with a local milk round, Lew Pedler is able to recall most of the people living in the 'triangle' from about 1947 until the early 1960s. Here are a few of his personal notes which capture some of the residents of Clift Road at a moment in time:

Frederick Knowles and his son Arthur (Frederick was Lionel Butt's uncle). Taken around 1910 possibly at 'Craigmoor', Clifton Wood.

Dorothy Butt taken on August 12 1934 by her son Lionel, probably at Weston-super-Mare.

Dorothy Butt, taken around 1939.

No 2: Mr and Mrs Short. I believe Mr Short was the brother of Captain Short, one time skipper of Bristol City Line and later of the Port of Bristol Dredging Fleet. Mr Short was the local National Savings Collector calling every Saturday for your shilling. Mother produced her savings book and Mr Short would accurately affix the stamp. The money was kept in a mottled black and white tin. Strange things one remembers!

No 3: Mr and Mrs Horler. Him tall, she short but very smart. Mrs Horler always wore green and her hat had long feathers.

No 7: Mr and Mrs Baynton and son Gerald. Gerald worked for Fowlers the motorbike people and always seemed to be riding the latest model which impressed us youngsters no end!

No 8: Mrs Miles. I never knew a Mr Miles. Mrs Miles was one of several ladies who always wore black. I seem to remember bunting, pictures and banners outside the house one day as a welcome home to her son, presumably from war service.

No 10: Mrs Avis. A quiet, slim and elegant lady, grey hair tied back and wore a long black dress and black shawl. Apart from collecting her milk or sweeping her front doorstep, the rest of her time seemed to be spent behind her closed front door.

No 15: Mr and Mrs Pike (Les and Dorothy) with Lionel, Bob and Stephen. Bob and I were the same age and spent our whole school experience together. He was my best man. Number 15 was always filled with classical music and Lionel was my piano teacher for a time until he went to university, or I got fed up with the practice – probably the latter!

No 16: Mr and Mrs Allen with two daughters, Maureen and Margaret, two attractive girls and although slightly older than us did not stop us youngsters allowing our ambitions to be exposed as totally unrealistic. If age was a barrier, class may have played a part too – both girls being privately educated.

No 22: Mr and Mrs Molyneaux and daughter Marjorie. The family came from Plymouth. Mr Molyneaux was a naval man who held a position on HMS *Flying Fox*, the training ship moored on Hotwell Road dockside near Mardyke Ferry.

No 28: Mr and Mrs Derrick. Mr Derrick worked as a docker, a big and burly man, salt of the earth and a gentle giant whose trousers were held up by a belt which struggled to operate, even at its limit.

No 32: Mr and Mrs Triggle, daughters Peggy and Sheila – later Williamson, husband Dick and son Stephen. I'm sure every street has a kid who always seems to be in trouble. That reputation as far as Sheila is concerned was me. Even to this day, Sheila [over 80 years old] will remind me of how Stephen, slightly younger than me, would rush back into his house as soon as he clapped eyes on me uttering the words 'There's that horrible Lew Pedler!'

Characters

The area appears to have had its fair share of 'characters'. Perhaps due to the proximity to the Ashton Court estate and Leigh Woods where trees provided shelter for people sleeping rough, several tramps seem to have frequented the nearby streets. Hazel Coles remembers one such person who was a regular caller at her house, usually turning up whenever her mother was out the front, sweeping the path:

> There used to be a tramp come down along Coronation Road called Sid Walker and he used to have a bicycle. Sometimes he'd come without his bike. He had little tiny silver glasses and he spoke quite posh. I should think in his time he was quite an intelligent chappie, you know, but he'd overdone his brain. Anyway, if Sid Walker was coming down, he'd look at [my mother] – you know, a bit strange and he didn't want to speak like. She'd say 'Hello' to him to him and then 'Just a minute' and she'd pop in and get him some cake, or if we'd had sandwiches she'd give him some and he'd go. Sometimes he used to come along with a lady called – well the children, we all called her 'Mary Pig Bin' 'cos they used to have little silver pig bins during the war like for scraps. Well, they used to go through the pig bins and we'd see Mary – she'd go along with these pig bins and of course her name [became] 'Mary Pig Bin' and she used to come along with Sid sometimes. They used to go over to Leigh Woods and there was another tramp. Yes, they lived in Leigh Woods, 'cos you didn't call them homeless in them days, they were tramps. And there was another one, and his name was Douglas. And he was more of a tidy tramp, you know and Mrs Williams, he used to bring Mrs Williams wood for her fires, because you know we used to have fires. He used to sit out there on a stool and chop the sticks for her ready for her fire and she used to have a special cup or mug for Douglas and he had a cup of tea and he had sandwiches or cake, and she always rewarded with like a meal. He was quite an educated man, like, to speak to and he lived over Leigh Woods with Sid Walker and 'Mary Pig Bin'. You'd see them in North Street and places.

John and Barbara Hickery also remember 'Annie Pig Bin' as well as other tramps:

> There was Annie Pig Bin. That was an old lady tramp. She was always in North Street. She was always known as Annie Pig Bin. She used to go in the bins. Dirty Dick used to live out in the woods. Yeah, so did Toby the window cleaner.

Most of the tramps had nicknames and David Ridley not only recalls one particular tramp but also finding the place where he lived in the woods:

> [I] spent loads of time in Leigh Woods, see the old tramp out there. I don't know if you ever knew he used to live in the second valley in a tin shed and he was one of the most educated people you could ever meet. He'd come pushing his bike up through North Street and the butcher'd give 'im all 'is ends and the baker'd give him summat else. Oh, he'd never have starved but oh, he was a dirty bugger. Old mac on, cap — but by all accounts his family originated from Leigh Woods, you know the houses up there and he was a educated person, but what turned him I don't know. No, we used to just call him 'dirty old tramp' 'cos you know what kids is, you could go out there, get up the top of [the rock slide] and 'is shack was down the bottom in the corner and you could thrown stones and you could hit the galvanised iron, but half the time he weren't there anyway. No, he was alright [but] he'd frighten you if he come towards you!

As well as tramps, the area had other regular visitors. Dorothy Pike remembers the time when the street lights were lit by gas which had to be turned on and off by a lamplighter:

> Of course we used to have 'Leary' coming round. D'you know the poem 'The day is nearly over and the night is drawing nigh, it's time to take the window to see Leary going by. For every night before you take your seat, with lantern and with ladder he goes walking down the street' — to light the lamp. Have you never learnt that poem? Yes, he used to run around with a long pole, and hitch it on and light it up with the lantern. And we had gales and the lamps went out, oh dear. Every night, in the darkness, and every morning to turn it off. Life has changed, hasn't it!

In the main, the people whose stories form this book recall those who shared their lives, whether close family, friends or neighbours, with more than a degree of fondness. As Hazel Coles says:

Oh, yes, it's happy memories of it all, and everybody was so friendly, so nice!

Chapter 2

SHOPS AND SHOPPING

He used to wear these leather leggings and he had a bowler hat and a brown workshop sort of coat and he used to have his whip and away the horse would go. He had a milk churn on the back – no crates. You could buy milk from his shop.

Mr Puddy the local milkman recalled by Lew Pedler

Imagine that you are a child growing up in the 'Ashton Gate triangle' in the early 1950s. The war is a recent memory and food rationing has only just ended. North Street is a thriving road with a wide range of shops stretching all the way into the heart of Bedminster. Within just two hundred yards of your home there are two bakers' shops selling bread and cakes made on the premises; several excellent cafés serving homemade cakes and ice cream; and three garages which as well as selling petrol and repairing car engines, supply paraffin – essential heating fuel in the days when few houses have central heating. In addition, the immediate area boasts a wool shop, dispensing chemists, a barber, seed merchant, newsagent, several public houses and off-licences and at least one sweet shop. 'Corner shops' stock fruit and vegetables, as well as a wide range of groceries in tins and packets. Most people shop on a daily basis and the larger local shops offer a same-day delivery service. Until recently, the local milkman used a horse-drawn cart for his deliveries and ladled the milk straight into your jug from a large churn.

What were these local shops like? Who were the people who ran them?

The toll house for the turnpike into Bristol. Long out of use as a toll house in this picture, in 2009 the building is in residential use. Note the tram behind the horse and cart, and the advertisements for beer from the Ashton Gate brewery which is just to the right of the picture. (Courtesy of Memories Photos, Bristol)

Let us take a trip around the area and learn from people who used the shops and can recall their owners. Times have certainly changed according to Hazel Coles:

> There was North Street with all the shops up through there you had everything up there, you didn't have to go anywhere else to go shopping really.

Down Coronation Road

Approaching Ashton Gate along Coronation Road from the city centre were three garages in quick succession:

> Before you make the sharp right-hand turn, on the left-hand side there was Warren's Garage and he did sell petrol, and he repaired bicycles and he sold paraffin – but of course he wasn't the only garage. Just a little bit further down at the bottom of the lane between Frayne Road and Clift Road was Sutton's Garage. That was a petrol station and that was the garage that I was always sent to for a gallon of

Henry (Harry) Warren's Garage on the corner of Coronation Road and Walter Street. Many local residents remember the petrol pump remaining on the forecourt into the 1990s. The building is dated 1888.

paraffin because I didn't have to cross a busy road or any road, it was straight down the back lane. It was two shillings I think for a gallon of paraffin. Farley's was there almost opposite Sutton's and again that sold petrol – so you actually had three garages within the space of a hundred yards all with petrol pumps although I guess Farley's, Warren's and Sutton's were really one-man shows. It is rumoured that the Beatles stopped at Sutton's for petrol following a show at the Colston Hall or Hippodrome somewhere in town. Certainly it was the rumour at school the next day but how true it is I don't know. (Stephen Williamson)

Many people remember the garages, the people who ran them and what went on inside:

On the corner was Warren's. Now it was a real muddle inside but he knew where everything was. If you wanted a little thing for something or the other if it was to do with a car or something like that, he would probably find it for you. And he sold paraffin because we were using a paraffin heater in those days, and he used to sell a lot of paraffin. (Mervyn Southway)

It was dark and junky in there. You didn't really go in the shop. There wasn't no room to go in, if you know what I mean. He used to sit just inside the door and he'd see to you and you'd pay him. Oh, it was all – well he didn't throw anything away. It was all paper and that everywhere. If there'd been a fire, he would have just gone up, y'know. But he knew where everything was, and he'd just sit inside the door and I can remember the petrol pumps being there but I can't remember when they stopped selling petrol, 'cos we always went in for our paraffin. He was always the same, Mr Warren. (Sheila Hall)

As well as running the garage, Mr Warren would turn his hand to most jobs, as Sheila Williamson recalls: 'He actually made my bike. Mr Warren actually made my bike.' Alma Chalmers also remembers the bicycles in Warren's:

There was a hand pump outside there and he sold bicycles, and mended bicycles. It was a smelly old greasy shop. And I'm told that he had a son that was called to the war and didn't come back.

Brenda Hatter also remembers the Warrens: 'There was old Mr Warren, Harry Warren, and then his son, Clifford, took over.' Mr Farley who ran the garage further along Coronation Road – 'a nice man' according to Sheila Hall – lived in a large house next to the garage premises. Lew Pedler also remembers both Mr Farley and his house:

Syd Farley – smashing bloke – never seemed to be oily but always in a brown coat when on duty. He had a deformed spinal condition. The house on this site was quite grand, pillars and steps at the entrance. Today it would have had a preservation order and survived.

According to John Hickery, Mr Farley

…was a very short gentleman. He used to take people round in a Bentley or Rolls Royce and he was 'humped back' and used to look through the steering wheel.

The former site of Farley's Garage is still used for car repairs and sales. Almost opposite Farley's was Sutton's Garage. The sign above the doors bore the name L B Sutton, the initials of which encouraged speculation by the local children:

> As kids, we used to call him 'Lord Button Sutton'. He employed two assistants, Jeff Bartlett who had black hair and always wore brown overalls and Len who was fair and wore blue overalls. I used to wander into the garage from time to time and watch the cars and engines being repaired. (Lew Pedler)

Next door to Warren's Garage stood The Elite sweetshop which was run by the Culblaith family, although Alma Chalmers recalls a Mrs Light running the shop at one time. Mervyn Southway describes the shop and some of its customers:

> [It] was a confectioners, a sweet shop – cigarettes and sweets. And the people, the chaps from the tannery, it was just across the road, they could go there to buy their cigarettes and sweets and whatever they wanted.

A short distance further on was Tommy Rowe's grocery shop which stood on the corner of Clift House Road and Coronation Road – 'Tommy's Corner' as it was known according to Stephen Williamson who was often sent to the shop as a child from his home in Clift Road. Displays of fruit, vegetables and other goods were piled high on boxes which filled the space at the front and the prices of the latest star buys were marked on the windows in white paint:

> On the corner, there was a shop there, sort of a general store. Tommy Rowe, his name was, and if you wanted anything you had to go and ask Tommy Rowe. And they'd say, oh somebody called in the night and dropped a few things, when things were very short, you know. You know, to get a bit of butter or you'd get a bit of tea, on the quiet. They shut that down when they made the road wider. He was on the left of the triangle. When they made the road wider they knocked his shop down. Or if they didn't knock it down they made it into a house or something. I know he disappeared anyway. (Dorothy Pike)

Tommy Rowe took over the shop just after his wife had died in 1954 and went to live there with his daughter, Sheila who was 15 at the time, and her maternal aunt, Eliza Jane Smith. Sheila has fond memories of her father:

Well his real name was John Grady Thomas Roger Rowe. He was always called Tom. Everybody knew Tommy Rowe! Every day he'd go down the market to get the goods like. He was always nice. He always saw a lot of people and he knew everybody, my dad. He was always jovial like, you know. He used to have a big forecourt and he used to put the boxes out with stuff in you know, and made that whitening up and put it on the windows the price of the things.

She remembers what it was like inside and some of the goods on sale:

You went into the shop – you had the front door next to the person who's there now [299 Coronation Road]. That was our front door to go in, but the shop door – there was a big window across there and then you had the shop door like at the end. And he sold all different fruit, vegetables, cheese, tinned stuff – everything like! People used to come in and ask for 'pinky fruit'. That meant like anything that was just starting to go. That's what they called it, 'pinky' fruit, you know, when it's just on the turn like. They wanted it cheap, and it was usually the posher people who wanted that!

A friend and members of Sheila Hall's family outside the shop of her father Tommy Rowe. The pictures were taken in the late 1950s. Sheila remembers her father mixing the white window paint from powder.

Sheila also recalls the flat behind the shop in which she lived with her father and her aunt:

> We had a room downstairs to live in but what you called your 'front room' like, was upstairs. There was three rooms – bedroom, bathroom and the front room like, you know.

When the shop was demolished in the 1960s as part of the scheme to improve traffic flow in the area, Sheila moved into a house almost directly opposite where the shop had stood and, amongst other possessions, took her father's piano with her. She recalls the difficulty they had getting it out of the flat:

> He had a piano and my brothers didn't want it so I said I'd have it and they had to bring it on a special thing across the road like. They had to cut the top of the stairs off so they could put the piano down easier to get it across the road!

Sheila remembers what it was like further on along Coronation Road, just past Farley's Garage, where the extension to the Toll House now stands:

> There was a shop down there and a rank of houses. It used to be Greenland's. She used to sell wool and patterns for knitting – and the daughter used to live in Clift Road. She was a nice, pleasant lady. I used to do some knitting and if I went wrong, I'd go down and she'd show me how to do it.

Mervyn Southway also remembers the shop:

> Now going on down from that garage where the – what do they call it, where the place is, down to the roundhouse? There was three or four cottages there, little cottages, and in the last one was a wool shop, a little wool shop – Mrs Greenland.

Living close by in Clift Road, Peggy Triggle found Greenland's very handy:

We did a lot of knitting in those days and we were always going there for coloured wools. We knitted all through the war, jumpers and cardigans or things like that – everybody knitted in those days. So we did a lot.

More or less opposite Greenland's on the corner of Clift Road where it meets Coronation Road, was a bakery:

Many years ago when I was going to school it was a bakers, but it was at the back, he baked at the back and I can remember going there and getting cream buns. That's all he did was in the baker's at the back. (Brenda Hatter)

Peggy Triggle remembers the shop and buying 'seven cakes for sixpence and you'd get an assortment.' Jantzen Derrick who, as a boy, helped out on a milk round and was rewarded by the milkman: 'He always used to stop there for a bag of stale cakes in the bakers.'

Other people all remember the wonderful smell of baking bread and the sight of delicious cakes on sale:

I can't remember the name of the shop but for most of the time that I remember it, the shop wasn't open. They had a bake house out the back, a two-storey building which was out here. The shop was on the corner and you went in and you could buy buns – cream buns, penny buns, anything like that – and he would bake hot cross buns. Wonderful! They were wonderful hot cross buns and they were warm and you could go and get them early in the morning. (Janet Steel)

As we were going to school in the mornings, mum would give us a penny occasionally and we'd have a treat and we'd knock on the wooden door, 'cos the shop wasn't open, and open it and go in, into the bakery where the bread was all coming out and the doughnuts used to smell beautiful! And we used to have a hot doughnut which was supposed to be for our lunch, and instead of that we was eating it when we were going to school. And the bread – beautiful! (Hazel Coles)

At one time, the bakery was run by Edwin Stubbs: 'He never had a tooth in his head did Ted. He was Ted to all his friends and everyone who knew him.' His wife was called Bertha and their nephew, Eddie Beavan, used to go and help out in the shop during the school holidays. Eddie has many happy memories of the time he spent there:

This would have been about 1951. I would have been about six then. My aunt and uncle had no children of their own so they sort of looked forward to having me for a fortnight, I suppose. I used to go down and spend it with them in the shop. During the school holidays, the summer holidays – yes. They spoilt me rotten like, so I used to look forward to that!

Like Tommy Rowe and his family, the Stubbs lived 'above the shop' as Eddie recalls:

They had a room behind the shop, like a little living room there, and then you went down a little passageway and there was a room at the back. And there was a small passage that went off of that and it went out into the yard. And they had a little outside loo out there. I can't remember them having a bathroom, but in those days, the early fifties, it was the old tin bath in front of the fire and everybody bathed Friday nights so to speak! And I think there was two bedrooms upstairs – a big bedroom and a smaller one like, that I can remember.

Eddie has vivid memories of watching his uncle at work:

I can remember him putting the bread in the ovens 'cos he had like a great long wooden paddle to put the trays in, 'cos it was the tin loaves then, with the small round ones and the bigger ones, all different size ones. I would presume that would be before sliced bread come in 'cos it was all like bread you cut yourself. But I wasn't really allowed near the ovens 'cos he was frightened that I could have got burnt or whatever. I can remember him opening the door and putting these paddles in you know. [The shop was] just a big square area. The counters were in an L-shape. You came down two steps from the living room at the back down into the shop which had a little bell there – you could hear the bell when the door opened. And I think I can remember the old wooden drawer – not like a proper till – but a little wooden drawer with like recesses in for the change and stuff like that.

He had all his trays out in there on the side – all his cakes. I remember the cream horns and that, cream and jam, and the cream slices – ah lovely! I had happy times there really. I can remember the apron he used to wear – a big white apron – and after he'd done his bread, there was always little bits of dough stuck to the hairs on his arms. That used to really fascinate me – all the little lumps of dough over his arms like, you know!

Although Eddie was too young to do actual work either in the shop or the bakery itself, he always had a good time there during his frequent stays:

I was always made welcome. He would, if there was ever a little bit of dough or anything like that, he would plop it on the bench and say 'Play about with that.' A couple of times I think he baked it, sort of biscuit type things like and then [he'd say] 'Go and show aunt then. Look what Eddie has made' – that type of thing.

Eddie is certain that the shop was rented by his uncle and ceased to be a bakery soon after he stopped going to stay with his uncle and aunt 'round '55 or '56 I should think' when it was sold by the owner. It reopened as a shop selling blinds, the Stubbs continuing to live in the first floor flat until Eddie's aunt died in 1962. Brenda Hatter worked in the blind shop 'for a couple of years' and believes it was owned by 'a family called Pimm'.

Up North Street

Round the corner where the Toll House stands, just along the start of North Street opposite the former Ashton Gate Brewery, was another bakers run by a Polish man by the name of Zohrer:

[It is] now made into a house and it's on the corner of Ashton Gate Terrace. Well that used to be a butchers but in later years it became a bakers, and I think he was Polish and his bread was beautiful and you could even go round on Christmas morning and you'd get a new loaf straight out of the oven. Of course the thing is that he had no money, so in the finish, after some time, he had to pack it up because he had to pay for everything – the flour and that – before they'd let him have it. So of course he couldn't afford it; he didn't have the money – but he was a wonderful baker! (Mervyn Southway)

He used to make lovely bread and lovely jam tarts. They were nice and crispy, not like they are now – all sort of soft and soggy! And we'd go and get a hot loaf and go home and eat it – all the butter melting on it. (Sheila Hall)

Hazel Coles also remembers her mother fetching bread from Zohrer's bakery:

When we lived down Ashton Road, my mum one Christmas – I think the Christmas was over a long weekend and I know we had visitors coming to stay. She had the baby's pram – they were quite deep the prams – and they used to have like little, well they weren't cushions – slatty things. And she took them out and put a sheet, a white sheet in the pram and I went up to the bakers shop going up by the Toll House and I got 24 loaves of bread. Couldn't do that today – 24 loaves of bread! I suppose with a big family in those days like, you know, any stale bread you never wasted bread, you always had bread pudding and things like that because mum used to do a lot of cooking. That was how we had to live.

From what Mervyn Southway recalls, Zohrer's closed down when he was forced to pay his suppliers for flour and other ingredients before he received them – a victim of an earlier 'credit crunch' perhaps! As well as Zohrer's, there were several other shops on the same stretch of North Street:

Well on the corner, which is now a house, there used to be Tom Hoddinot, the barber. Then there was the lane, the Back Road. And then there was one, two, three shops. But the next one was a sweet shop which my aunt kept. Her husband was a Southway. They kept that sweet shop for some years. And then after that, Bet Thompson, Betty, opened it as a greengrocers. She eventually went to Canada to live with her daughter. (Mervyn Southway)

Yes, there was a barber's shop along there. There were three or four shops there – yes, there was a barber's shop there but I can't recall the name. (Peggy Triggle)

Rumour has it that Stan Laurel once had his hair cut in this barber's shop, presumably when he and Oliver Hardy were performing in Bristol – perhaps at the Bedminster Hippodrome. Dorothy Pike also remembers these shops well, most likely recalling them as they were pre-war:

> On the left hand side, a little row of shops. Well the first shop was a bakers – that was Aulman's. The next was a sweet shop. The next again was Graham's the paper shop and the end one was half a sort of chemist. She wasn't a registered chemist but she used to sell all chemist [items], and radios. On the other side, the shop at the bottom of Ashton Gate Terrace, was a butchers shop and then eventually that turned over to Stuckey's the outfitters and I worked with them for a while.

As a boy, Lew Pedler delivered papers for Mrs Graham:

> I used to deliver *The Green 'un* around the local area, but Sunday papers, morning papers and evening papers I used to deliver [as far as Ashton Vale] and Bower Ashton. She had quite an extensive round and was red hot as well for as soon as any new houses went up, she knew all about the neighbours.

Along Ashton Road

At one time, Ashton Road from the Toll House to Duckmoor Road boasted a number of shops selling a variety of goods, and a photograph taken in the 1930s shows a parade of smart shop fronts, each with a white sun blind pulled out over the pavement (see p.12). Several of the buildings here suffered war damage and Janet Steel believes that some of the shops nearest the Toll House were rebuilt as houses. Roland and Pam Reed who lived, as they still do, only a short distance away in Frayne Road, have clear recollections of these shops:

> There was a sweet shop – well, everything it sold, newspapers – Shrapnell's it was called and they took over two shops eventually. At the bottom [of Frayne Road] you had Day's. He used to supply whatever it was for Bristol City. He was a keen City supporter and Pam used to go down there and get bacon, ham. [We] used to get all [our] groceries there. Slightly to the right there was a newsagents. That was Hazel's.

Roland used to pop over at six o'clock on Saturday evenings to buy *The Green 'un* so that he could read 'a write up for the team I played for.'

Dorothy Pike also recalls many of the shops on Ashton Road as they were before the war, as well as what they sold:

> Oh we had it all down here. There was a row of shops. There was a sweet shop, a grocers shop, a fruit shop, a paper shop, a cycle shop – on the corner of the lane there. They took that down to widen it, for the motors to go down through. And there was a sewing machine shop there. A Mrs Ing kept that. And Gale's [Garage at the start of Duckmoor Road] sold oil, because of course we had oil lamps in those days, they sold the oil. And then further down was Gulliver's, who sold grain. The pub of course is still there [the Coopers' Arms and Rising Sun]. And there was a shop there that sold very nice cheese. And there was a cycle shop there as well. It was quite busy down there, really and truly. The dairy on the top of Bath Road, Bath Street. A dairy shop – they sold milk and cream and butter. And Marshall's, of course, they've always been there – that's a café further down again.

Jantzen Derrick and Hazel Coles who both grew up on Ashton Road also remember the shops there:

> The shops I remember, which again is opposite the park as I lived in number seven which was two or three houses in between the shops. From memory, there was a house on the very end which is the side where The Coopers' is, the pub. Then there was a replacement cleaners, a cleaning business, which I was very friendly with one of the lads there, Ted Possil. His dad ran the business there. Then there was a newsagent's shop, Hazel's. Then the other side was a grocers shop – I think that was called Day's from memory. And then you had The Bluebird on the end, which sold the ice cream and sweets and stuff. And that's my memory of the shops. (Jantzen Derrick)

> [First] the Bluebird, then the newsagents, then the café, go past there and there was a few little cottages, about three, and then there was a shop there and that was a grocery shop. We used to take our coupons up there [as] Mum was a cook, she always liked cooking and you couldn't get apples and things during the war. Anyway they used to do dried apple rings and all different dried fruits so we used to 'ave to take the points up and they used to cut them out the book. You

soaked them in water overnight, then you boiled them up and made an apple tart. I can remember that. And then I think it was the pub [formerly the Rising Sun]. (Hazel Coles)

The Bluebird was a prominent and very popular shop and being close to the park attracted a lot of customers:

Yes, the Bluebird, yes. I remember the Bluebird well. I know as boys, as we went down to the park, or came away from the park, we'd go in for a 'halfpenny cornet' – ice cream cornet. Yes, I can see that man now. I can't remember his name, but I can picture what he was like – a tall man, you know. I don't know what his name was. Yes, we used to go in there for sweets, ice cream – he made lovely ice cream – and we used to go across the park to play football. (Mervyn Southway)

Many people still recall the ice cream which was made on the premises by the proprietor:

It was beautiful ice cream! And it was always milk – and it was always in a wafer. And very often, talking about my friend, Mr Pearce would go down and buy us all a wafer. That was a huge treat! Oh yes – it was a treat. (Peggy Triggle and Sheila Williamson)

As a child Janet Steel, who lived on Frayne Road within sight of the Bluebird, was great friends with the owner's daughter, Paddy:

Well, I know for a fact at the bottom of Frayne Road, the first one there was a café – a sweet shop – the Bluebird. The ice cream was wonderful! He used to make his own. He had a little place built on the back where everything was made and transfer it, mixed…oh it was beautiful! It was milk powder and eggs and lovely wonderful things went in ice cream then. Super! When we were eight, nine, ten, eleven…oh yes, we ate him out of house and home with ice cream! I remember rationing on sweets was still going because my grandfather, he had a thing about Fox's Glacier Mints and we'd be up there and he'd say 'Paddy Crocombe', so she'd say 'Yes Mr Amesbury?' 'Here's some money. Go and get me half a pound of glacier mints.' And she used to say: 'Where's your coupons?' and he'd say 'Oh don't worry about things like coupons! Here's the money for my glacier mints.'

The Bluebird was run by Vic Crocombe and Janet recalls the café being a favourite meeting place for players from Bristol City Football Club:

Vic Crocombe used to host meetings. It was a gathering place because you could sit at a table and have a fizzy lemonade with a dollop of ice cream in it or something like that and all the City players used to congregate in there and their manager would be in there and they would wander in and sit down and have an ice cream or what have you – so Mr Crocombe used to keep getting sold shares because they had no money in those days. He'd say 'Vic, I really need a new centre forward, or something. Would you like to buy some shares?'

Just beyond the Bluebird café was a newsagent's shop:

Frank Hazel was a newsagent. I think he was next to what is now the Red and White Café and then I think there were two houses before Ken Day the grocery guy. Hazel's was the newsagents where my dad got the papers from and we called in every Sunday on the way home from church to pay the papers which tended to be a discussion about the previous day's football, you would see the same sort of people at the same time and dad would meet some of his mates and you could be in there about half an hour really having a chat, but it was a handy little sweet shop and newsagents, you would use it quite frequently to buy a penny's worth of sweets in those days. I can't remember how long they remained there certainly mid-sixties I would have thought maybe even later. (Stephen Williamson)

The Bluebird was one of several cafés and tea rooms on Ashton Road:

Further down, on the corner – more or less on the corner of Duckmoor, was Marshall's Tea Rooms. Now they used to keep all the goal posts for the pitches at the park, so when a team came down to play there, they got the goal posts from Marshall's, took them over to put them up themselves. Nobody put them up for them. Then they'd come back there and have a bath in an enamelled bath.

And Marshall's used to sell halfpenny pieces of what they'd call 'Chester cake'. (Mervyn Southway)

Dorothy Pike also remembers the Chester cake, as well as the connection between Marshall's and the footballers who used the park for their games, just as today's Saturday matches:

I used to buy Chester cake from Marshall's at the bottom of the road here, down where the shops are. That was very well known. They used to use that for the football. The footballers used to go there and change.

A third café, run by Mr Urch, stood on the corner of Baynton Road. It seems likely that this building suffered bomb damage and was demolished to widen the entrance to Baynton Road.

This was further along here, after the Bluebird, perhaps where that glass place is now, Hicks – they provided meal. Everything for dogs and all that – dogs and horses. Mr and Mrs Hicks. Very posh people they were, and they had a daughter, Margaret. (Peggy Triggle)

Home deliveries

As times have changed, so have shopping habits, and delivery rounds made by horse and cart were once commonplace with 'two horses and carts going round'. (Janet Steel)

The coal was delivered – of course we were fortunate because we had a back lane. And the fruit was delivered, we had a very good man who came with fruit. The bread was delivered, the milk was delivered. (Dorothy Pike)

The Triggle sisters lived with their parents in their grandmother's house on Clift Road:

Well you see my grandmother didn't need to go out at all. The milkman [Mr Puddy] came. He had his shop where you could get cream, which of course obviously we didn't really have in those days and milk – and the horse, on that corner over there [Clift House Road]. So Mr Puddy came; then Mr Clements came twice a week with the horse and cart with the green groceries. His actual name was Clementa. The coalman came and as you know, we had a coal house and a pantry in the kitchen and the coalman would come every fortnight or month and come in the back way which was lucky and then come and put your coal in the coal house so that you had plenty of coal.

Mr Puddy the milkman was very much a local character by all accounts and operated his dairy business from the shop which was later owned by Tommy Rowe. It seems that he stabled his horse in a shed next door to the grocery shop: 'It was quite a big place because he kept Dolly his horse there.' (Peggy Triggle)

Mervyn Southway also remembers the stable:

Puddy the milkman used to keep his horse in there. That was just where he kept his horse. I don't think he done the dairy work there. I think it was just the place for his horse – I think. It's like if you have a car, you'd have that for the garage. He had it for a horse!

[Mr Puddy] had this horse and cart and delivered to all the local ladies and they took their jugs to him and it was ladled out to them. (Alma Chalmers)

According to Dorothy Pike:

[Mr Puddy] used to leave the top off [the milk churns] to let the rain in. And the milk was covered with hairs from the horse! It's true – honestly. He used to ladle it out, that's what Fred Puddy did.

Lew Pedler, having grown up in the area, assisted with another milk round from 1948 until 1952 or '53, the milk being supplied by Hawking's Farm at Bishopsworth:

The delivery round was quite extensive since the milk van didn't arrive until 10 o'clock [at night] and the delivery round commenced at 7am. The 'milk girl' was Joan Vowles – a jolly red-face country girl who originated from Churchill and landed up at Hawking's Farm as a Land Army Girl. On Saturdays and during the school holidays, I delivered the milk and collected the money. The country was still subject to rationing and any extra coupons for sweets were given to Joan who generously shared the spoils with me and sixpence pocket money for helping. I was also trusted with eggs although one day disaster struck. Rather than take three or four trips from van to front door, I put a couple in my trouser pockets. As I stooped to place the ones I had in my hand in the dish, I heard a crunch and then felt a very wet leg! Anyway, after that, I always carried eggs in my school cap. Although milk was in bottles, it was still sold direct from churn to jug if customers required it.

Hazel Coles remembers milk being delivered in this manner, the 'poor girl' perhaps being Joan Vowles:

They used to come along with a big milk, well, like a bucket thing, and they used to have the ladle and lift the pints of milk out and put in the jug and I don't know how the poor girl carried it because she used to have this big wooden thing over her shoulders with milk hanging down, so heavy.

Hazel is certain that one of the 'milk girls' employed on a local round was called Mabel Smith.

Lew Pedler recalls other forms of home deliveries:

There were always the general grocery deliveries. I remember there were two or three guys used to come round with those bikes with the big baskets on the front. I used to go to school with quite a number of kids who had Saturday jobs at a very early age.

Local suppliers were very keen to please loyal customers, sometimes literally going out of their way to retain regular orders as Janet Steel recalls:

Mr Gittins [who lived at 14 Frayne Road] was the grocer. He had a grocers shop in North Street, I believe it was number 242, but I'm not absolutely certain. They used to send somebody round to the house and take the order and then they would deliver your order and the next week you would pay for the order that you got the week before and place the new one. And when we moved down to Tickenham, Mr Gittins still delivered [our] order — all the way to Tickenham! And to keep us going, he used to send us a packet of envelopes, a packet of stamped envelopes, to send our order back in. Oh, they were incredible, they really were.

Further afield

Alma Chalmers and her aunt, Hazel Coles, both remember Bessie's, a corner shop in Walter Street that sold the beer from the cask:

The ladies — and it was mostly the ladies that I remember — used to go for their half a pint of 'mild and bit' with their jugs. They would leave it till just before Bessie was closing her doors and then they would chase up the road to be sure that it was fresh when they poured it. That would last till she opened again next morning and it would start all over again. She was a large lady. I think she was a spinster — I can't ever remember there being anyone else in the shop except Bessie. Whether she'd inherited the shop from her parents or something. But that's all I can remember about her. It sold nothing else but booze and lemonade! Nothing else was sold there. I don't remember spirits, I only remember the beer. I did go in there once — for my grandma's half a pint of 'mild and bit' and my mother was so cross because I wasn't really allowed to do that kind of thing. (Alma Chalmers)

Hazel Coles tells of the occasion that she was sent to Bessie's by her uncle to buy his beer, even though she was under age:

So I put the jug on the counter and I said to Bessie. 'A pint of bitter please', never had to ask for bitter before because my dad didn't drink. Anyway she said 'Ten Woodbines?' I said 'Yes please.' Never had the beer 'cos she couldn't hear and she thought I said ten Woodbines. Lovely! So I took the jug off the counter and paid for the Woodbines. So my uncle said, 'Where's the beer?' So I said, 'Oh no, she's so stone deaf she thought I said ten Woodbines.' So he had his Woodbines and no bitter.

The necessity of shopping locally on a regular basis may also have been convenient, but had its downsides for children as Stephen Williamson well remembers:

Mum used to shop three days a week in North Street, Monday Wednesday and Friday and until I was school age I wasn't left in the house alone although my grandmother was there, was taken to North Street three times a week where we went to the shops. In those days you went to the greengrocers, the ordinary grocers and you went to the butchers and there was also a Co-op there, where I still call it Smiles whatever that shop is now. So that was a regular Monday and Wednesday trip. Friday [we] had to walk a little bit further because there was a fresh fish shop past the Hen and Chicken, just before where Cashsave was there was a fresh fish shop there and Fridays, although we were not Catholics, Fridays was traditionally fish days so it was a little bit further walk on a Friday. I think I was quite glad when I did go to school because I no longer had to shop three times a week!

Shopping habits have changed over the years. The appearance of the first supermarkets in the 1960s and the growth in car ownership saw a decline in shopping on a truly local basis and most of the shops described in this chapter have long since disappeared – changing hands and now selling other products or having been converted into houses and flats. Dorothy Pike neatly sums the situation up: 'Of course it was the big stores that upset them, ruined them.'

Chapter 3

PLAY

Knock out ginger – we used to try that by linking all the knockers together, never very successfully!

Lew Pedler

Many of the people whose life stories make up this book have clear recollections of childhood games and other adventures they enjoyed in the years before or just after the war. Stephen Williamson vividly highlights one of the main differences between then and now:

I think perhaps one of the most memorable things growing up and playing in the mid-to late-fifties was that you played in the road because there was no cars. To imagine Clift Road without cars is impossible. I couldn't tell you the guy's name but there was a guy at the bottom of the road had a car and that was about it. My father eventually acquired one in 1957 I think but until then the road was clear.

Mary Butt remembers the 1950s and '60s when her three children were growing up in Clift Road at a time when there were generally fewer cars on the roads:

Children were let out to play at a very early age and told to 'stay on the block' or up and down the lanes [alley ways behind the houses].

Lew Pedler also grew up in Clift Road in the years immediately after the war and recalls various street games which he and his friends played:

[It was] brilliant in that we had the street to ourselves. Yes, the Bobbies used to come and tell us off for playing football in the street but we played football in the street anyway! We used to play football against the garage doors which are technically there on the side of the road at the bottom of Clift Road, on the left hand side as you look towards Coronation Road. That was the perfect goal and we used to play football against that and run the gauntlet if anyone bombed the ball across the top. A lot of football was played in the street, very little traffic. Marbles and that was a work of art in the gutters because of course the gutters were cobbled. I can remember distinctly one day after school playing marbles in Ashton Drive and it was a dream because you had concrete gutters and the marbles ran true! Cricket we used to play in the street as well. That used to frighten the neighbours right, left and centre and Bob Pike took out a window in Clift Road and I shall always remember it. I bowled, he hit and there was a smash – all seemingly in stop time! I stood back in amazement and the next thing I saw was a pair of legs disappearing round the top of Clift House Road. He charged around the back into home. I sort of scurried out of the way quickly but got caught by Queenie Yeats and we had to repair the window.

Janet Amesbury ready to roller-skate with 'our gang' around Christmas 1947. The photo is taken outside 8 and 9 Clift House Road, near C Bond warehouse. Back row left: to right Patricia (Paddy) Crocombe, unknown, Janet Amesbury, Brian Baylis, Dorothy Williams of 31 Clift Road
Front row left to right: Peter Hanlon of Clift House Road, Gregory Rogers of 6 Frayne Road, unknown brother of back row unknown, Ian Bryant of 20 Clift Road

Another popular pastime for children in the post-war years was roller skating. Lew Pedler remembers the noise made by the metal wheels on the surface of the road and pavements of Clift Road, and an 'exclusion zone', which one resident established outside her house to keep the worst of the racket at bay:

> We were roller skating in the street. It was metal wheels in those days and it used to clank across the street. We could come down as far as number 30 and no further and that was it. If we ventured any further, oh that was trouble!

For Hazel Coles, living up on Coronation Road which was busy with traffic even before the war, meant that play was generally restricted to the safety of home:

> We weren't allowed to go into the street much but we used to make our own fun in dad's garage and we used to have a fun fair there. We used to have a roll down penny table and darts, with Roger Bush and Pat Bush and Brenda Baylis.

The alleyways which run behind the gardens also provided ideal places to play:

> We were lucky because we had the lanes. We could use those for hiding, so hide and seek and stuff like that was always going on using the lanes as sort of shelter. The actual houses with their walls and steps gave you cover as well and when we knew the neighbours weren't about, we used to hide in the gardens anyway. (Lew Pedler)

The nearby park was the perfect place for local children to go with their friends. Greville Smyth Park, Ashton Park, The Park – whatever name it goes by – is a much-loved and well-used local resource. When asked about the various names, Janet Steel was very clear: 'Yes, Ashton Park. Nobody ever called it Greville Smyth. We always called it Ashton Park.' Hazel Coles agrees: 'Yes, we called it Ashton Park.'

At one time, the Council employed a small team of men to maintain Greville Smyth Park in good condition:

Greville Smyth Park was clearly popular for pram-walking. Here we have in the right-hand picture Stephen Williamson (aged about 8 months) in the spring of 1951, and in the left-hand picture Tina Hall (Sheila Hall's eldest daughter) in the left-hand pram with her friend Deborah (possibly McGough), in March 1963. Both pictures were taken by the tennis courts, the left one showing Frayne Road in the background, and the now demolished wooden shelter.

Back in the fities there were three or four, the main one being a guy called Len Sladen. Well, yes I mean most people worked five and a half days a week then whether there was a bit of a shift because there were two or three younger people who helped him whether they did a shift. It's difficult to remember if they were there on Sundays. It was an obvious presence they had their own hut or shed which was obviously their base. You go in from Frayne Road and if you were going to take a straight line to Al's Tikka you'd go along the top by the railings and just before you drop down to Al's Tikka opposite what are the changing rooms now, sort of round clump of trees, and right in the middle of there was where their shed was. (Stephen Williamson)

As well as tending the flower beds, mowing the grass and carrying out other tasks on a regular basis, the park keepers served another purpose as Stephen remembers only too well:

Up until recently you could still read 'Cycling Prohibited' in this park at every entrance, written in white letters in the gateways. And of course now they've made it a cycle way through it's great, but as a small child on a three-wheeled bike, no problem, but as soon as you progressed up to a two-wheeled bike you were not allowed to ride in Greville Smyth Park and it was enforced. The park keeper would enforce it, just as he would shout at you if he saw you in the flower beds or climbing a tree or doing any other things that you weren't supposed to. Again the fact that mum and her sister had a dog they were in the park twice a day [and] I always knew that he would be saying 'Hey, your Stephen was riding his bike in the park today!' so you had a bit of respect in those days, I think, for people like that. We used to grumble about him, I suppose there was the odd occasion you would try and ride your bike and get away from him or whatever.

Janet Steel also remembers that she and her friends held the park keepers in awe:

They had a park keeper. He didn't stand any nonsense so there was never any vandalism as such because if you put a foot wrong, he'd have you and he'd give you one round the ear you know. You'd hear him saying to the lads, 'I know who your father is' and if he ever did get in touch with your father, you were in trouble!

John Hickery agrees:

If you did get up to anything, they'd be straight on shouting at you and getting you out of the park.

Like many municipal parks, Greville Smyth has evolved and changed over the years, as Dorothy Pike recalls:

Well of course there was the park. And I think it was used more then – and that park used to be absolutely beautiful. Along where you live [Frayne Road] – the bed along there, the flowers right the way down, it used to be an absolute dream. And in the bowling green they had the most beautiful roses, I don't know if they still have them. They had the most beautiful standard roses. Absolutely glorious, they really were. And there used to be a toilet, an underground toilet. The bowls house was by the toilet – by that flowerbed. They moved it over to where it is now.

Michael and Peter Phillipson, with Janet Amesbury in the centre. Taken around 1940 in the Phillipson's back garden in Frayne Road (no 19?).

Stephen Williamson on horseback, aged about 18 months old, around 1952. Taken in Stephen's back garden, 32 Clift Road.

Gertrude Babbage of 11 Frayne Road with Janet Amesbury, aged 4-5 years. Taken around 1940-41, in front of the air raid shelter in Mrs Babbage's back garden. Janet tells us that Mrs Babbage and her husband George lived in the upstairs flat and the Pont family lived in the ground floor flat of no 11 [Miss Gwendoline Pont lived the latter part of her life at no 21 Frayne Road].

In spite of living nearby, for some children the park might as well have been a foreign land as far Stephen Williamson was concerned:

> The park. I couldn't tell you what age, but until I was a certain age, the park was sort of forbidden ground. Fine to go over with mum and dad or my auntie but not on my own and I remember being allowed to go in the park alone [for the first time] but I couldn't tell you what age. I was allowed to go in the park and just stay in the top by the tennis courts for half an hour or whatever and then gradually it moved on from there and it was the same with my own children when they played on Gores Marsh, behind where we live now.

The park has always been well used. David Ridley remembers how busy it was:

> In my day, it'd be packed out down Ashton Park, be packed out down there. On a Saturday you could go down there and there'd always be loads of football matches and things like that going on. You didn't have the children's play area, you just had swings and a roundabout – that sort of thing, but I mean people used to walk round there with their prams and go round there with their bikes more than they do now. That was very busy at one time.

At one time the swings and other play equipment were located in a different part of the park, as Jantzen Derrick confirms:

> And then you had all the swings, and the play area was at the top end of the park obviously they've cut through with the road [Clift House] now – all the swings and playthings were up there. Clift House Road ran along the top, but down over was all the play area there, with swings and stuff.

Other people also remember the swings being closer to the river:

> When I was first allowed in the park the swings were at the bottom of the first slope by the Frayne Road entrance under the curve of the flyover, because that curve of the flyover wasn't there until the mid-sixties until they built the Cumberland Basin

Sheila Hall (with a child whose name she can no longer recall) in Greville Smyth Park around 1957. The photo is taken in front of the flower bed, by the park entrance at the bottom of Frayne Road. Visitors are asked to keep off the grass.

scheme. You walked down a very similar hill just inside that first entrance and there was a steep sided slope up to what was Ashton Avenue and the end of Clift House Road with the swings and roundabout and slider in there. The slopes were covered in bushes and they made a wonderful playground you could get in and out of them and build dens and play hide and seek and all the sort of things we did in those days. But then of course with the building of the Cumberland Basin several bits of the park were taken for the road and the swings were moved to their present location. (Stephen Williamson)

I played in the park yes. I can remember going in the park as you went in Frayne Road entrance you went straight down the slope and the swings and all the roundabouts were down on that part just a concrete thing 'cos I had an accident down there. I was on the merry go round and somebody caught my leg and that was where the swings were, I can remember going down there, I was quite young. There was an American [soldier from a nearby camp]. He borrowed a bike and he wheeled me home 'cos I couldn't walk – my cousin was in charge of me and he was only the same age as me. I must have been nine or ten probably still p'raps, during the war. We just played in the park anyway. We had no problems. (Brenda Hatter)

And the park – they used to have the swings and that were right up at the far end of the park with all trees round it. (Sheila Hall)

John and Barbara Hickery agree:

When you go down that slope from the top of Frayne Road the slope at the bottom, that's where all the swings used to be, on the right hand side. They took that with the road.

As well as identifying ways in which the park has changed over the years, many people have fond memories of times spent there:

…and Ashton Park, well, the kids used to live down there really. They took a lot of it off for that road and yes they [the swings] were down the bottom. On a Monday, I used to go down to Jennings Court, and take Alma's mum Kath over to Ashton Park and 'cos she loved Ashton Park 'cos she was about 16 and she met her husband – girls and boys used to go out together when they started work, and they used to meet in Ashton Park and that's where she met her husband. Yes, and she loved Ashton Park. We used to sit there and reminisce, you know how it was. (Hazel Coles)

Brenda Hatter's children Julie and Martin, in Greville Smyth park in September 1963. In the background is Frayne Road.

Karen Thomas in Greville Smyth Park, with Frayne Road behind. Those interviewed often spoke of the park's fine flower beds. Taken in September 1967, not long after Karen had returned from working in America.

One of the pre-war features of the park was a prominent swimming pool which was situated on the west side, near Ashton Avenue, now the dual carriageway – 'More or less where they've put a couple of goal posts, sort of five-a-side posts in the last couple of years – more or less where that was.' (Stephen Williamson)

It was handy for Stephen's mother and aunt when they were children growing up in Clift Road as 'the gentleman who lived next door was in charge of the swimming pool in the park' so they remember the pool well:

> My father took me the first couple of times and put me in the shallow end and told me what to do, you know, and helped me swim. And then I started to swim, but I never went to the deep end. I was a little nervous – apart from the fact that it was very cold! (Sheila Williamson)

No one is really certain when and why the pool was demolished but it seems that it fell into disuse during the war. Sheila again: 'I'm not sure – I don't think there was a bomb there. I'm not at all sure whether it was bombed.' Hazel Coles has a similar recollection: 'I think it was the war, I think it was closed 'cos of the war. And then they never repaired it and demolished it.' Janet Steel remembers it always being 'a ruin – it was all boarded up – never did see inside it. The building was there but we never saw inside it, no.'

Once boarded up, the pool became a source of fascination – especially for the local boys:

> One of the big mysteries in the park was always the swimming pool. There was a large red brick swimming pool which had long since had the door ripped up and I always wanted to see what was inside because I guess I had a vision of it still being something resembling a swimming pool. A very large rectangle of red brick – four red brick walls, obviously making up a rectangle – completely open, and I always wanted to see in there. Well I did. I started following, quite naturally, Bristol City Football Club in the early sixties and in the mid-sixties they used to train in the park the first team would train on occasions in Greville Smyth Park, and to those of us who used to pay on a Saturday, or every other Saturday to watch the

team, it was great to go in the park and literally stand alongside your heroes. They used to train on one of the three football pitches and they quite frequently would kick footballs by accident over the swimming pool. One morning, I was down there watching them and they'd obviously decided it was time they collected some of their footballs back and somebody was sent over to the football ground to get a ladder which they then put up to the top of the parapet. Well that was an ideal opportunity to see in, wasn't it! Once they were in and looking around for their footballs inside, it was easy to climb the ladder and have a look over. Tremendously disappointed! It was all overgrown and weedy and brambly. It was obviously just a concrete mess. I think as they began to knock it down they made holes in the walls and again you were able to see through. I think as a lad I would have loved that to have been a swimming pool in operation because Bristol South was the nearest. (Stephen Williamson)

Len Hatter had a similar experience:

I can remember playing football in that park and I think it was Ken [Hall?] – he lived in Raynes Road couple of doors from us – kicked the ball and it went over in the pool and we couldn't get in so I got on to my father and he went somewhere. I believe it was down off Jacobs Wells Road. He had to go there and get somebody with a key to come open it up and get the football back.

Losing a football over the wall seems to have been a common occurrence. John Hickery remembers climbing over the 'fairly spartan walls about four feet' to retrieve his. As budding footballers, Jantzen Derrick and his friends used the sides of the disused pool as 'goal nets', but had to cope with retrieving the balls that were kicked over:

We used to play against the swimming baths because there was a big swimming baths on the far side of the park – an outdoor swimming pool. It had obviously been open before my day. It was all shored up. But I must admit I climbed in there quite a number of times to get footballs and what have you which we kicked over the top. We used it really as 'goal nets'. It was quite a big pool – red brick.

Jantzen also agrees that the pool had ceased to be used for swimming 'well before [the war]. It was up there for a long time. I'm not sure when it was actually dismantled, but it was there for a long time, all through my childhood.'

Other facilities in the park have survived almost unchanged for many years, the best examples being the tennis courts and bowling green:

Yes that's always been a bowling green, for years. And a tennis court, I've played tennis there for many hours. The tennis courts were very nice then. Wednesday mornings, we used to book it for two hours and it was always very nice, very pleasant. (Dorothy Pike)

But tennis courts – that's a good thing, I would think that the school runs it. We used to do games. I went to Southville Secondary Modern, up in Beauley Road and we used to come to Ashton Park. In our last couple of years there, we had a tennis club at school and we used to come down there with just one teacher and we could go on the courts there because we used to run our own. So yes, we used to spend a lot of time over there. (Janet Steel)

Below. Back, left to right: Edna Thompson, Janet Amesbury, Kathleen Cook
Front left to right: Pat Crocombe, Dorothy Williams, Pam Pearce, Phyllis Roberts

Above. Janet Steel writes, 'Friends and neighbours who enjoyed playing tennis and helped us youngsters to learn the game'. Taken in 1949 in Greville Smyth Park, which, as Janet reminds us, 'We always called Ashton Park'. Back left to right: Dorothy Williams of 31 Clift Road, Kathleen Cook (nee Gillard), Pat Crocombe, Phyllis Roberts of 17 [?] Frayne Road. Front left to right: Edna Thompson (nee Popham) of 19 Clift Road, Janet Amesbury, Pam Pearce of 9 Frayne Road.

Not all days in the park were for sun and tennis. Karen Thomas took this photo in December 1965, which she describes as, 'The 'second lake' taken from the corner at the end of Frayne Road, near the current traffic lights, before the flyover. Flooding due to continuous rain'.

Like the swings, the tennis courts at one time were situated 'at the bottom of the park. They were that horrible red stuff, you know – that dusty stuff.' (Sheila Williamson)

As well as playing tennis as a school activity, Janet and her friends also organised their own tennis club in the school holidays. The park also boasted a bandstand. A photo of it exists, but views differ as to exactly where it stood:

> We played a lot on the bandstand which was a concrete base, quite big in the centre of the park and they always had a bandstand on there; then later on in years they took it down and we used to play football a lot on there when the weather was poor. (Jantzen Derrick)

The original use of the building which now stands rather forlornly on the high ground in the park was a shelter for park users, as Stephen Williamson recalls:

> Of course the other thing the park had was a shelter. It's still there but they bricked up the front of the shelter and knocked through from the changing rooms to create a bigger changing room for the bowls with a big wooden mahogany bench which went all round it and obviously if it came on to rain and you were in the park you

could jump in the shelter. Probably 20 years ago that disappeared and knowing some of the problems that go on in that park and other parks you just couldn't have an open shelter like that today. In fact I had a short spell of playing bowls, not in the park [teams] but I did actually play in there once or twice in recent years and was very conscious that I was in the old shelter again as you obviously go in from the bowling green side now.

The large, flat, grassy space on the west side of the park has always been used for a variety of purposes:

Mr Jones our sports teacher would march us down in crocodile fashion to the park where – well there weren't posts as such I suppose we carried a couple of poles whatever to make it realistic and of course I remember we arrived there one day to find some young trees had been planted so that must have been 1960, '61, '62 – some time about then – right on the area where we always used to play football on! I guess we just moved – the park was big enough. We never played on the actual football pitches. The three football pitches that they still use nowadays I believe have been there from my childhood. (Stephen Williamson)

Stephen Williamson also remembers being taken over from Ashton Gate Primary School for sports days and recalls a particular incident which befell him:

The park was used for sports days. A classic story was: I certainly wasn't winning the race but I was doing quite well and as a treat my mum and dad bought me a packet of coloured Polos, as they were in those days, and they fell out of my pocket and I stopped to pick them up!

The park has always been used for team games, although the amount of use has perhaps declined over the years. Lew Pedler remembers football being enjoyed by different groups of people each playing on different days:

I can always remember that football ground being a football ground for different classes of people. During the week, because there were workers in North Street, there used to be a congregation of blokes, probably in their twenties or thirties playing football on there at lunchtimes. Saturdays of course it was clogged up with football players and the crowd watching as well. Sunday mornings it was always the older blokes, the blokes who'd done their National Service. Sunday afternoons it was our age group.

Lew also recalls games of cricket in summer with his friends, the brothers Clive, Tony and Barry Hussey-Yeo:

Their grandfather was Billy Wedlock. They always seemed to have a cricket kit – they had the wickets, bats etc, so it came to a point where we used to play cricket and Mr Yeo used to come across with us as well and sort of coach as such and we spent a large number of evenings in the park playing cricket with all the kids in the street. You used to get a situation where kids from other streets would say 'Can you raise a team and we'll play you?' and of course the pitches were always marked out in the park as well. Latterly, when I was about 12 or 13 – that's when we formed a core of a football team called the Ashton Wanderers and I've a feeling that Jantzen [Derrick] was involved in that as well because Jantzen, Bob [Pike] and I were all in the same class together. So you can imagine that if you had Jantzen on your side, you sort of sat back and watched it!

Roland Reed was another keen footballer and cricketer who played in the park on a fairly regular basis:

[My team was] Exeter United – nothing to do with Exeter. There was a Wolverhampton Wanderers junior club and our captain eventually played for Crystal Palace. The problem we had in those days was the allocation of pitches. I played in goal. Going to Exeter United wasn't a good move for me because they were so good.

Roland remembers German prisoners-of-war being allowed out from the nearby camp to play football against local lads in the park. One of the prisoners, Alous 'Alec' Eisenstrager, was a talented footballer and Roland used to joke about competing with an 'international player'! Alec remained in Britain after the war and played for Bristol City Football Club for several seasons.

When it came to cricket practice, Roland and his friends used the wall of the disused swimming pool as a 'wicket'. 'I always remember hitting the ball on a car that went along and the lady wouldn't give the cricket ball back.' Roland prided himself on hitting the ball hard as it was quite a distance from the pool to the nearest road!

Hazel Coles recalls the visiting fairs which were set up on the level ground directly opposite the house where she lived:

What we used to do then was after the fun fairs had all gone 'cos they had fancy beads and that all hanging up, all round the things and when they went away, they used to leave pulling down all the things, the beads used to fall off on to the grass and we used go over there, collect the beads to make our necklaces. We used to have really fun times. Well, when the war was sort of ended, yes. [My brothers and sisters] were quite young then. I don't know – well, I should think my youngest sister was perhaps about 18 months old I s'pose when we used to push the pram over there with them in to collect all these things.

From tennis to toboganning; this picture was taken in 1966 by Karen Thomas from her balcony in 32 Frayne Road.

When it snowed, the long, sloping bank which runs across the centre of the park from north to south provided the perfect place for sledging:

> I suppose the best time in the park was the winter of 1947, the really cold one, yes, when you couldn't go to school because the pipes froze so you had to stay at home. Everybody had a toboggan and you took it over to Ashton Park and you stayed there from crack of dawn and after dark [when] you took your bicycle over and put your bicycle lamp propped it up against a tree and illuminated the runway. And all the children were there – plus a lot of grown-ups used to come in the evenings as well because there was one gentleman I can remember had one of these wonderful [ones] – ours were sort of wooden sledges or the tea tray or something like that – and he had one of these beautiful, high, lightweight ones and he could go right across to the old swimming baths on his! Oh yes – it could really go, down over. Yes, wonderful times. Oh it was a bitterly cold time – yes, it was wonderful! (Janet Steel)

Hazel Coles recalls how the Williams children acquired their sledge. Their father was a taxi driver:

> He always used to go up to Warrens and get his petrol and that was how we had our toboggan. Because Mr Warren's son came home and they were talking and it was snowy and that and he said, 'I got a toboggan'. And he went in and got the toboggan and gave it to my dad and it was a proper little toboggan. It had proper runners and as I said, over Ashton Park we used to go and we used to have races over there with the toboggans and my eldest brother, well, there was like four of us used to sit on this little toboggan, squeezed up but we did and my eldest brother was always in the front like – you know – and we used to go up towards the top, and then come down.

Hazel also remembers the incident when she and her brothers were challenged to a race over the snow by a man with a beautiful sledge – quite unlike the home-made affairs generally used by children in the park. At the bottom of the bank was a small wall which, if struck in the right way by a sledge would add speed to its course and help it across the field:

Some hobbies were carried out close to home. Here is the garden of William Amesbury, 12 Frayne Road, in 1936. Janet Amesbury explains that the garden won a prize, and that the greenhouse was full of carnations, the growing of which was Mr Amesbury's hobby.

There was a feller came one night and of course this little toboggan we had had these metal runners and we used to go – oh – whizzing down over 'cos the snow had sort of iced you know. And there was this man came and he had this great big wooden toboggan which he'd made – oh, a big posh thing you know. 'Cos we was all there looking at it, you know and he said 'Right' – 'cos we were always the winners. 'Right' he said. 'You won't be winning tonight.' So my brother said to me 'I don't think we will because – look at that, such a big showy thing!' So of course, he said 'Right, all get on your toboggans – line up now.' So of course we gets on ours and all lines up and we went down over the hill and I can see it now, we went down over the hill, we hit the – well my brother said if we hit the wall, we're all right so we're going down and we're all leaning down 'cos we're going to get down to the little wall and we hit the wall and we went right out through, nearly to the swimming baths and we looked round and he was still up towards the top! And my brother said 'I told you'. So of course we were dragging our toboggan back and going up and he said to my brothers 'I bet you won't win tomorrow.' So my brother said 'I'll bet we will!' But we didn't get home till nearly 10 o'clock that night and my mother – oh, we had to be in by seven – my mother she was frantic and she said 'Right, that's it. You won't be going out tomorrow!' So of course we couldn't go out, could we, we were going to have this race. That's right, 'cos it was dark, it was so dark in the park, there wasn't a light in the park 'cos it was wartime like, we couldn't have lights on. But this little wall, like going down before the bandstand, if you hit that you seemed to skip right over, and there was four children on that toboggan mind! No, it seemed that we just landed and went on, no accidents, it was wonderful, I'll never forget that. We were barred, we couldn't go.

The same slope was also used for fun of a different sort by Lew Pedler and his friends:

It was always necessary to have a trolley of course, means of transport, and everybody used to try and purloin pram wheels or whatever. We had our trolley, a nice little sort of thing on the back and very useful on Bonfire Night for collecting things and pinching things. On one year, I do remember on a very, very cold Saturday afternoon filling that cart with leaves, setting fire to it, running down over the hill to Ashton Park – you can't do it now, it's all fenced off – and we gathered so much pace that we had streams of smoke pouring out the back of it and we charged across the football pitch and it was already foggy and we just added to it. They could have killed us because you couldn't see anything. We actually filled the whole place up with smoke. Ran the gauntlet with 22 angry footballers wasn't funny really!

Just as nowadays, the park provided an ideal meeting place. Barbara Hickery describes what she and her girl friends got up to:

We just played in the street when we were younger and then all met up. Came down North Street and went to the park watching the boys. There were girl gangs too and there used to be gangs of boys.

In recent years, thanks to the efforts of a very active support group – the Friends of Greville Smyth Park – the existing children's play equipment has been refurbished and a lot of new equipment purchased to cater for children of all ages. The future of the park as an asset for the local community seems assured.

Chapter 4

'COME ON YOU REDS!'

We've always been a 'City family' – living over this part.

Mervyn Southway

The red-and-white grandstands of Bristol City Football Club dominate the Ashton Gate area and no one who lives in the vicinity can ignore the presence of the club, especially when home matches are played and the surrounding roads are packed with cars. In spite of pre-war photographs showing Clift House and Clift Roads lined with supporters' cars, the majority of fans in those days travelled to the City ground on foot or bicycle. The Williams family who lived near the entrance on Ashton Road decided to provide storage space for bikes:

When we moved there Ashton Road by the football ground, the chappies all used to come down to the football ground with bicycles and there was an old man, well, elderly man, used to stand over by 'Fatty Wedlocks' and he used to tell them to bring the bicycles over there. Anyway, this particular day, my dad said 'Tis a shame all those bikes – those poor chaps they just throw them down.' Cos we never had a garden there – well mum used to call it a yard, but it was like a cemented thing at the bottom, you know, and a pathway going down. Well he said 'I think I could put the bicycles in there. I think the man across the road charges them to put the bikes there but he stands there and watches them.' So anyway, that's what they done. They decided that they'd open up the gates and put the bikes in and dad said 'I think we'll charge them like a threepenny bit.' You know, three pennies in the old days. 'And we'll have to give them a ticket to say that that's their bike.' Of course mum was all worried about it, you know, and anyway they started it and my brother used to stand there on the Saturday and take the money and they brought the bikes in and it was packed with bicycles and we never had one stolen – not one – and never any fuss. They were in and out and gone in no time. And when you think about it like, if there was a good match coming, they'd have five or six bikes wide and sort of all on top of one another, but they were never all over the floor or anything, they were all stood up and they used to come in and move their bike, like, and take their bike, put them back and gone again wonderful! (Hazel Coles)

Not even the most ardent City supporters were able to attend matches on a regular basis. Alma Chalmers' father worked in the tannery on Coronation Road:

The guys in the tannery worked a six-day week for quite a long time, and then that was reduced to five and a half days and it was then that they could go to the City ground on a Saturday afternoon. [That was] going back quite a long time, probably in the late forties I should think. They would still have been working a six-day week at that time.

As a boy, Lew Pedlar remembers being taken by his father to watch amateur football matches played in Greville Smyth Park, opposite the entrance to the City ground, by teams called Ashton United, Victoria Athletic and Ashton Athletic.

As far as Ashton Gate was concerned, as soon as I was given free rein, then I used to go to Ashton Gate. We were lucky because [it] wasn't the enclosed ground that it is now. Our fun and joy was [to get in free!]. We used to watch [the players] train as well and afterwards we used to collect their autographs. A lot of them in those days lived in Hotwells so we used to be playing football in the afternoons and the City players would be coming through and sometimes they'd joyfully join in and we had to try and tackle them – well, we had no chance!

Jantzen Derrick, who played for Bristol City from 1958 to 1971 and who still lives in the Ashton Gate area, left school at 15 and joined the club 'on the grandstand' – the equivalent today of being an apprentice pro:

> You cleaned the dressing rooms, swept the pitch, swept the litter from the steps and generally done all the work round the ground really. You did the general work on the ground, and then when we'd finished our jobs we could train and practise afterwards.

He played his first match for the first team when he was 16 – some feat when he recalls the average age of the players at that time being about 25.

> When I made my debut for the City, I was about sixteen and a half-sixteen and three quarters. It was not a debut as such. They chose me because they wanted to

Jantzen Derrick in the Southville School Senior Football XI 1956-57
Back row, left to right: L J Brown, B Bennett, R Garland, R Derrick [not related to Jantzen], R Lane, J Hartnell, B Dowding
Front row, left to right: R Pow, B Pratt, B Britton (Captain), J Kennedy, Jantzen Derrick. The school was in what is now Ashton Gate Primary School, with an annexe at the end of Raynes Road, fiittingly behind the Bristol City ground.

Three national youth sporting stars in 1958, all from the same year at Southville Secondary Modern Boys' School!
Left to right: Keith Smith, who played for England School Rugby, John Nash who boxed in the British Finals 1956 and England v Wales 1958, and Jantzen Derrick, who played football for England. Keith lived next door to the Ashton Gate Toll House, John in Greenway Bush Lane and Jantzen at 2 Frayne Road.

win some games and we were fighting against relegation in the second division and I got chosen to play. But it wasn't the fact that they were only going to give me a couple of games and drop me out, just to give me a taste of it. They actually thought I could do something to save them.

Jantzen always loved playing football: 'I played for the junior school and strangely enough, the guy, the school teacher that did the football team at Ashton Gate Primary School – Mr Jones – he's still alive now.' Having played for the Bristol Boys' Team, Jantzen was selected to play for the England Schoolboys' Football Team when he was 15:

In those days you only had one cap. Five games I played and was sub on one of them, but you don't get a cap for one game, you only get a cap for the whole lot. That year was a particularly successful year as far as the England Schoolboys' was concerned because usually one or possibly none might make the grade as a professional footballer, but that year there was Terry Venables, Peter Thompson – you might have heard of – played for Liverpool; a lad called Ian Wilson played for Preston for quite a long time. There was Alan Harris who played for Chelsea – his brother was Ron Harris, 'Chopper' Harris. Aidan Williams who was my colleague in the Bristol Boys' side, he played a few games for the first team in the City. So it was quite a successful team. Ronnie Boyce who went on to play for West Ham for ten or twelve years. So it was an exceptional year.

The England youth team at Watford Football Club, April 19th 1958. England won the match that day against Ireland 3-0, and Jantzen Derrick scored a hat trick, although he admits he missed a penalty kick! The talented England side included several players who went on to have notable careers. The players here include: [back row, first players left to right] Bert Murray, Alan Hardy and Terry Venables, all of Chelsea; [back row last player on the right] Peter Thomson of Liverpool; [front row, first players left to right] Phil Chisnell of Manchester United and Ron Boyce of West Ham United; [front row, fourth and fifth players left to right] Aidan Williams and Jantzen Derrick of Bristol City.

Jantzen clearly remembers getting ready for his first match:

When I was selected for the England Schoolboys' side, mum and dad had to kit me out for the trip and they never had any money. They used to get the clothes from a shop up in the Gloucester Road — just this side of Zetland Road — and they used to pay, I don't know how much — five bob a week. And I went up there and got kitted out with a double-breasted blazer, grey flannel trousers, black shoes and a white shirt and off I went on my trip — my first trip. A big adventure, yeah. Funnily enough it's amazing, as Bristol was a little outback — a little country town in those days — and when I got there I was the only one with a double-breasted blazer. The likes of Terry Venables were in Italian-cut suits because they'd come from London! I felt a little bit — well that's how it was. And that's how mum and dad kitted me out for the trip.

We played about six games. We played Scotland at Wembley, the old Wembley Stadium which was a fantastic occasion. I think that day, from memory, there was eighty thousand there! Probably 60,000 kids and 20,000 parents. And then they played Scotland at Ibrox up in Glasgow. We played Wales at Watford. Ireland somewhere else. What used to happen is that when you used to play, you had to be chaperoned by a school master. The school master would take you on the train and make sure that you get to the stadium or whatever.

When he first joined Bristol City, Jantzen was paid £2 a week working for the ground staff. Once he began to play regular games, his wages were increased, but not to the levels that professional footballers enjoy nowadays:

When I signed my first professional contract at 17, I think from memory I was on about 'eight and six'. What they mean by that is eight in the winter and six in the summer. So when the end of the season came and you're in the summer months, you drop right down on the lower amount and you've got no way of earning any extra money because in the season, you can earn – I think in the early days it was £2 for a win and £1 for a draw, on top of your wages, your eight. And you might have £2 appearance money in the first team. Then if you're in the top ten positions in the league, you will be paid according to that: you might get an extra £5 – I'm using those figures because obviously if you're only earning £8, they're not going to give you five! You get so much for being top of the league and then it's graded down so you might end up, if you're in sixth position you might get an extra 50 pence a week or something like that. And that's how it worked. So consequently, in those days, I and the majority of the lads, most of them, went and got little jobs in the summer, so when I finished playing – the Cup Final was usually the first Saturday of May – and then you'd have to report back for training probably the second or third week in July, so you'd have a reasonable break, and because you obviously went down onto the lower money, I always worked in summers.

During the summer when football ceased for a few weeks, Jantzen worked for Honeyfields driving seven-and-a-half-ton trucks which were garaged in Stillhouse Lane, Bedminster. The company had a contract with the British Aircraft Company and Jantzen would drive to Filton each day where he and the other drivers were detailed for specific jobs. Jantzen recalls other City players of the time:

The best, I mean for me – everyone knows John Atyeo. John was the great player, a great player. He was in the side long before I got there. John died – he was only 62 or 63 when he died. I suppose John would be ten or fifteen years older than me…ten, but a tremendous player! What he'd be worth now, I don't know. He was obviously an extremely good player when he was young and he played for Portsmouth in the first division when I think he was about 17 or 18. And City were in the third division and Harry Dolman went down and persuaded his dad to sign for the City as opposed to Portsmouth. Whether Harry crossed his palm with silver at the time or not, I don't know. In some ways it's because you had maximum wages then. Up until about '62, '63, no player I think, to start with, could earn over about £20 a week. They then increased it to £25; then the maximum wage was abolished in about '62, '63. I think that was George Easton and Jonny Haynes. John Haynes became the first £100 a week player. So I suppose in some ways there was no reason for him to play in the First Division because he wouldn't be earning any more money than he would be. But in all fairness, most players want to play in the top level and John [Haynes] – he stayed with City all of his career and he played for England when they were in the bloody third division! He played four of five times for England; he scored the goal – I think it was against Ireland – to actually get into the World Cup, but then he never got chosen for the World Cup. But a good player – a big lad, six foot two, a big strong lad, but never used his strength in that way really. Lovely, lovely control. He scored goals – he could score goals.

Having played with Bristol City from 1958 to 1971, Jantzen joined Paris St Germain in what was then the French first division. After one season, he and his family returned to Ashton and he ended his football career playing for Bath City:

I've had a great life, but I suppose, on reflection, if I could have my time again, when I was 15, when I left school, I was courted by all the big clubs. Mum and dad didn't want me to leave home. I was offered sort of ground staff, apprentice pro, by a number of big clubs – Arsenal, all the big clubs really, and I could have chose where I wanted to go. Bristol City was a club I'd supported as a lad, my dad was a City fan and my ambition really was to play for the City.

Jantzen later discovered that West Ham United had made an offer for him when he was 18:

> They offered twenty thousand, which was a lot of money then – you could buy a semi-detached house for two grand then, you know, so it was a lot of money – and the City turned it down. They had a good side then, the West Ham one – they had Bobbie Moore and 'Hurstie'.

Football training routines were very different in those days and after the summer break, the players needed to regain their full fitness as quickly as possible and prepare for the coming season:

> In all fairness you do relax a bit from the break from May till the middle of July. I'd put on a bit of weight, but I could stand it at that age. And then, when you start back to the grind, you'd start – 'cos in those days it was…the training was different really, because I can remember the early days was certainly – the first day was always a bloody cross-country run from the ground, up over Rownham Hill and all round the 'seven mile wall' and back round, you know. And that was it really. It's funny how things change, you know, when you start talking like that. The trainer's name was a guy called Lemmo – Len Southway – and he played for the City for a long, long time in the pre-war years and he was an old guy when I went down there, Lem. He was the trainer then, and then he became a kit man. He was down there for bloody years. Funny – in those early days, in the sixties, his philosophy was keep the ball away from you, the lads, through the week, so they'd be hungry for the ball on a Saturday – which was a load of cobblers! I've never heard anything more ridiculous in all my life, really! And I mean – you should have the ball. But that was how it was. You'd do your – you'd crunch into your pre-season training and within two or three weeks, you'd be up to the mark, and then a few pre-season games and then into the season proper.

Mervyn Southway has special memories of 'Lemmo' whose real name was Len:

> I don't know why they called him that. He was always Lemmo in all my time. He was my uncle, my father's brother. Now there were – I think it was four brothers and three or four sisters – but Lemmo was the one that played, went professional. All the rest played football, but in the amateur line. In fact there was a time when one team – I think they played for Yatton at the time – the team composed of all the Southways, a couple of my mother's brothers and also, my auntie's husband who was a Stenner, they all of them were in the same team! And they got the same medals. Lemmo got on well with everybody. Now he always used to wear a trilby because he was conscious about his hair. They all used to have a lot of fun in those days, footballers. There was none of this 130,000 a week. But they all had fun as well and they say when the young uns – you know, like he was – one of them would come along and be larking about and knock [Lemmo's] hat off. He'd go wild because of his bald head. And he didn't totally believe in doctors. If he had any aches and pains, they used to say then that he would get a soaking wet towel and he would beat his self with this towel to get rid of it, rather than go to a doctor.

When Lemmo finished playing for City, he went to Switzerland as a coach and then returned to Bristol:

> Then he came back to the City again and of course he was too old for playing then so he came back then as what they used to call a trainer – and a kit man and all the rest of it. And he was down there, altogether – by the time he finished with Bristol City – for 50 years.

Lemmo was regarded as a local character. He lived on Dampier Road and drove what Mervyn Southway describes as 'an old banger'. Mervyn recalls an incident involving Lemmo and his car:

> D'you know, many years after he'd finished with football and he'd lost his wife – and he'd also lost his daughter and he also lost his son. And he'd go up North Street and if he wanted to go in the grocers, he'd go up North Street and the

cars would be parked on the side. He'd just park by the side of them and go in the grocers! And I know there was one day when there was a policeman came in: 'Whose is this car outside?' 'Dunno.' So the policeman went. After he's gone, Lemmo would get in the car and the policeman said 'Who's this car?' So Lemmo said 'I don't know.' He said 'I dunno!'

In spite of his eccentricities, Lemmo was quick to spot a talented player:

There was this Roy Bentley, an inside forward, and [Lemmo] thought the world of him. He said, 'I don't know which is his best foot.' He could kick with both feet. And the Wolves come down there one day and [their] supremo was Major Buckley. So he said to Major Buckley before the match: 'Keep your eye on our inside forward, Roy Bentley, and let me know what you think about him.' So after the match [Lemmo] said 'Well what do you think of him, Mr Buckley?' 'Not a lot,' he said. [Lemmo] said 'Get your notebook out and put Roy Bentley in it. He'll play for England.' And he did. He played for England!

Mervyn used to get free entry to watch City matches, walking into the ground alongside his uncle. 'That didn't happen all the time – on the odd occasion!' He describes some of the great players of the time, as well as matches played in front of a capacity crowd:

I saw Stanley Matthews play down the City ground when he was an up-and-coming player. He was 18. I think at the time I was about 10, and they had an evening match against Stoke City for Ernie Brinton – that was the wing half for the City – for his benefit. Stanley Matthews played in that match. Now I seen Ernie Brinton when the City were in the First Division, some, a few years ago, and unlike a lot of these footballers who, once they've finished, they don't want to know it – he used to go to the City ground. And he was ever so short and he was stood behind the goal on a stool, on a wooden stool, 'cos he had to! And I spoke to him afterwards when I were a-going out, and I said 'Yer, Ern.' They were on about in the paper Stanley Matthews played down the City ground in so and so. I said 'He played long before that, didn't he? He played for your benefit.' He said 'That's right.' He said 'Do you know how much I got for that benefit?' I said 'No.' He said '£25!' Yeah, yeah, yeah!

I also remember when the City played Portsmouth in the Cup. Portsmouth were a good First Division team and they drew at Portsmouth and they had a replay on the Wednesday afternoon at the City ground. Now, in that match they said – and this is before the terrace, before seats – they said the gate was 42,000, but there was well over 50,000! The gates to go in – where people were rushing to get in, broke the gates down. Around the pitch, some of them, with the crowd there, surging forward, they broke the rails down and they was stood all along the touchline – not all of them of course, but a lot of them. They played Portsmouth – must have been 1935. So of course they were stood on top of what was then The Shed – it's now a stand – right on the top of there. There must have been a hundred people stood on the very top! And they let us out of school early to get home before the crowd, so what did we do? Went down the City ground! The gates were open of course, so we went in and we happened to get somewhere where we could sit on something and look at it – and we seen the two goals scored and they won two nil! But there was all that many people there.

Although home matches today might not enjoy past levels of attendance, Bristol City Football Club has a strong following of loyal supporters. In 2006, the club was promoted to the Championship League and nearly succeeded in reaching the Premiership the following season. Having had its home at Ashton Gate since 1900, the club plans to move to a purpose built-stadium in Ashton Vale in the near future.

Chapter 5

GOING TO WORK

Two of you would be in the pit and you'd have to shovel the waste flesh up into barrels – great big wooden barrels – run it round the 'dock', take it in. They'd open up the furnaces and they used to burn it. The seagulls, they used to eat loads of the flesh and we had rats like bloody dogs in the boiler house!

David Ridley describing working in the tannery

Ashton has been described as Bristol's first industrial suburb. Until the first part of the twentieth century, a number of coal mines were dotted around the south west edge of Bristol – such as those on Dean Lane, and South Liberty Lane. For over a hundred years, south Bristol – Bedminster in particular – was synonymous with the cigarette industry, WD&HO Wills being the main employer with an empire of factories and offices. Cigarette production required, and supported, numerous other businesses, such as the manufacture of cardboard and the printing and production of cigarette packets. Until cigarette production largely ceased in Bristol in the late 1980s, employment opportunities were numerous and a job with Wills was considered a job for life. There are examples of several generations of the same family being employed in various jobs with the company at the same time.

In this chapter, people from Ashton Gate describe their experiences of work, both in this part of Bristol as well as elsewhere. Kath Winter recalls her first job working for one of the biggest print firms in Bedminster, as well as the work which her husband and father did:

I worked in Mardons when I was single and then I went back [after I was married] in the restaurant. I was making the cigarette packets. When I first got married Maurice [my husband] used to drive for them and they used to take the casks of tobacco to deliver that and there was one further round and there was one in Winterstoke Road. Pop was a sheet metal worker and on the Sun Alliance [building on the Centre] there used to be a big sun on top the building and Pop did that. He also done the work on the top of the University at the top of Park Street.

Mervyn Southway's first job was close to home, working in a relative's shop on North Street:

When I left school at 14, I went to work temporarily in my aunt's and uncle's butchers and greengrocery shop, taking out orders on the bicycle, but I didn't intend staying there. [Their name was] Tanner. The greengrocers – my aunt took it over because my mum's mother and my aunt's mother had the corner shop which is now a restaurant, opposite the Hen and Chicken. They had a big nursery at Yatton, half way to Weston, and two of the sons used to work the land. It was a massive nursery, something like about 15 greenhouses, big ones. They use to grow all the veg and send it up to the shop. They didn't go to market, it was all freshly dug. Then my aunt eventually took over, only in another shop opposite and I worked there. My dad said to me one day, 'What do you want to do my son? Do you want to work in a shop? Do you want to work in an office? Do you want to have an apprenticeship?' I said, 'Well dad, I'm very keen on figures.' I said I'd like to go in an office where I was dealing with figures and all that sort of thing. So he said, 'Right. Work for a big firm. The job's safer.' A couple of nights later, he said 'There you are, there's a job there, look. Bristol Tramways and Carriage Company. Get your pen out, write for that.' So I wrote the letter to them and I had an interview [and I asked] 'Well what is the wage?' – bearing in mind I was earning about 15 shillings or £1 a week in the shop. They said 10 shillings a week – 50 pence now – so I said 'Well do you mind if I have a word with my dad?' You know, because in those days, your dad was the man; you always looked upon him, for guidance. So I went home and spoke to dad and I said 'Here dad, I've got the job, but it's only 10 shillings a week.' He said, 'I'll 'phone them in the morning and tell them that you're starting.' So on the Monday, I started. Clerical work – all clerical. There was a time when I was on the comptometer and all things like that, you know – and figure work. It was a massive great big thing with masses of numbers on them. You could add on there and you could divide on there. [It was a computer] more or less.

When it came to moving from job to job, having a particular skill was a definite advantage as Dorothy Pike recalls:

I went to Merrywood School, Merrywood Secondary then that was. I was there for four years. Then my father fell out of work, there was that terrible depression, and so I left school a year before I should have done really and took up a job as a shorthand typist and I was a shorthand typist until I married. I worked in Redcliffe Street, Frank Burroughs and Sons. Motor Factors they were. I went to the Greggs School, down in Wine Street. It used to be Fry's Factory there, down the back, I can't remember the name of it now. It was the De Beers School I think they called it. I learnt Greggs shorthand and typing. That took me through. And I was glad of that, because when Lionel [my eldest son] went to Oxford, I was very glad of my knowledge then. I went to work at some clothiers down at – Stuckey's actually, you've heard of Stuckey's haven't you? The shop at the bottom of Ashton Gate Terrace was a butchers shop, and then eventually that turned over to Stuckey's, the outfitters. I went to work for them for a while, I was a typist there and then they moved out to the other end of the town which was too far for me, so I went over to Redcliffe and did Farley's office work for them and worked for 15 years over there.

Mary Butt also worked at Farley's Garage on Coronation Road:

My mother-in-law [Dorothy Butt] didn't approve of [me] going out to work, but when [my daughter] Sylvia was 16, I asked to do office work at Farley's Garage and worked part time. I had a break when Phillip came along and then he went to school and I worked there again. That's how I got to know Dorothy Pike. I did petrol accounts every month.

When she left school and began work at the age of 15 in 1954, Shelia Hall also learned a specific trade, as a seamstress:

I was a machinist — apprentice machinist, sewing dresses and things. Leonard Lane. That's near the Centre. You wouldn't know it's there, really, Clare Street and then you go up there, and then there's a lane and there's factories behind there. I went as an apprentice. German Jews as bosses and he always had a pipe in his mouth with his lip curled down. It was a funny name — Schwartzers or something. My dad had to sign a form for me to be an apprentice and [the boss] asked me his name and I said 'John Grady Thomas Roger Rowe.' He said 'Don't be silly! You take this home and ask him to write it properly.' And he apologised when he seen that it was his right name! I was very quiet in those days. I was apprentice there and then I went to, out Stokes Croft, sewing again, but more capes and things for abroad.

Sheila's father ran a grocer's shop and she could have been working there:

I did a bit, like when I was home. I used to enjoy it, but my auntie who looked after us when my mum died, said 'You need to go out and meet people.' So as I said, I went to the sewing jobs. And the last job I had when I became pregnant was out St George. So I've never been round this way working — I always had to get buses.

As well as making a way in the world and bringing in some money, starting work gave those who had had little school education the opportunity to develop as a person, as Peggy Triggle describes:

I was a very peculiar, mouldy, thin little creature — you couldn't call me anything else! And do you know what really was the making of me? When I was 14, after I left school — I'd had no schooling at all — I was sent up to do shorthand typing, and for some reason I was sent right up to Whiteladies Road. So I had to walk up — what's the first hill? Yes, Clifton Vale. Then through the Bird Cage, down another long road, across Whiteladies Road to a little tiny road where I did shorthand typing. I did it for about 18 months and that seemed to be the making of me going up to Clifton. Because mother always would liked to have lived in Clifton. This would have been about 19… it was before the war — about 1938? Yes, about 1938, I should think. I seemed to be alright after that. I first worked at a fish oil place, a horrible little place in Queen Square. I don't how I came to go there — it was a funny little place, not nice at all. I don't know why they had fish oil places.

After that I went to a greengrocery place in Queen Charlotte Street. Then I went into an insurance office in Baldwin Street and I was there quite a while. Then just before the war, I went back into Queen Square into Holder Brothers who were to do with boats and things. I didn't have to be called up or anything. I worked in there till just after the war. I was a bit cross because the weather was bad, the war was on and you were expected to be in work dead on time – we always were. And just once, I was late, he was really cross about it, he was really nasty to me. So I decided I wasn't going to stay there after the war and then I went into Rigby and Eden's in King Street. I was 27 years in there and that was it.

Working in the tannery

It is understood that a tannery has been in operation on the Clift House Road site since the middle of the nineteenth century, serving as an important employer for the area. Kath Winter married into a family with a tradition of working there. Her husband's grandmother 'died of cancer and they said they picked up terrible diseases working in there. They always said it used to be terrible years ago cleaning those hides.'

As a child, Brenda Hatter (née Baylis) lived in a house on Coronation Road near the tannery and describes how several generations of the Baylis family worked there during the first half of the twentieth century, in some cases living on the premises:

The Baylis family connection is there was my grandfather William Baylis, my grandmother Suzanna Baylis and they had three sons – George was my father, William and Frederick – and two daughters Elizabeth and Catherine and they lived in 2, Tannery Cottages. These were the two little houses that are just to the left of the main entrance and in later years they were used as offices I think. They lived there 'til I think it must have been about the turn of the century [1900] and then they moved to Ashton Gate Terrace. My grandfather worked at the Tannery all his life. He did retire but then he went back again and he stayed there till he was in his seventies, which was round about 1950. I don't know exactly what his work was, something with the leather, and my uncle Frederick he worked there all his life as well.

Stephen Williamson grew up in the 1960s in a house directly opposite the tannery and remembers witnessing the routine of the working day, as well as an incident which involved the family cat:

> Two memories of the tannery. One was they had a siren which called the people to work at – let's say half past seven in the morning – again at quarter to eight and then again, I think at eight o'clock for the start of work. It went again for coffee break if I recall and again at 12 o'clock for clocking off and those sort of times. It maybe didn't go three times but it certainly went twice in the morning, once to wake people up and once to say – right, time to start work. I guess in the early fifties a lot of people lived locally to the tannery. The other interesting bit was, we had a cat called Smokey because she was a grey colour, and she disappeared for a week. When we eventually found her she was a dark brown colour and we had to change her name to Susie and we were 99 per cent certain she'd been in the tannery and fallen in one of the vats and got herself tanned! Yes, Smokey turned to Susie.

Thelma Short, also grew up opposite the tannery, in a house in Clift House Road:

> Many Italian prisoners-of-war worked in the tannery and from my bedroom window they could be heard singing in the mornings.

Alma Chalmers was brought up just before the war in one of the 'two up, two down' terraced houses in Walter Street which her parents, Arthur ('Art') and Kath Payne, rented for six shillings a week. As far as she can recall, her father worked at the tannery for over 50 years:

> It was very hard manual work. I remember Dad coming home to change after falling in the pit where the animal carcasses were treated. His money was stopped for the time that he was away from the site! His overalls would almost stand up on their own [because of the chemicals that impregnated them]. How my mother ever managed to launder them, I don't know.

By comparison with Alma's father, the thirteen years that David Ridley worked at the tannery seems a short spell. His grandfather, who owned a farm out at Cleeve in the 1900s, moved to Bristol as one of three foreman for the firm of Thomas Ware and Sons. David recalls his grandfather being an expert in dealing with pig skins which were used for handbags. Both David and his brother followed their father to work at the tannery in the 1950s and David provides a very clear account of what the work entailed and the various processes involved in the production of leather.

I don't know if you've ever been in a tannery, but there's a lime yard so when the skins come in — we had them from Argentina, South America and local but all of them come in on lorries and you had to sort them down into great big piles in the lime yard. Then they went into pits. First off it would be like 'chloros', that was to clean them, then you'd move them from pit to pit different strengths with lime to burn the hair. Then they'd go through what they called a scudding machine [to] take all the hair off and all the flesh off the back. They'd then go onto what was called a rounding table where they'd be cut into what the two sides would be bellies, this end would be the shoulder and the rest would be the hide for soles. The belly and the shoulders, they were a softer leather so they were used for more things like belts, shoe uppers and bags and all that sort of thing. Then it was a process of pits, then what they call the tan yard and they'd go from strength to strength, right through weeks and weeks different tanning to obtain the colour and the texture and everything else, ending up upstairs in the driers. Then they'd be buffed or rollered whatever they were going to be used for the specific things and then you had a warehouse where they'd be bundled up and shipped out to different areas for the process of whatever was going to be made of them.

Nothing was wasted during the long process of producing finished hides, as David recounts:

When the hides came in, nine times out of ten the ears would still be on and sometimes the hooves. What you got to remember is, when they went through the processes and through the final machines there was no wastage. All the flesh was put into big containers and wheeled out on the 'dock' outside and tipped and the seagulls would come round and they'd take loads of it. [The rest] used go along the end of Bedminster Parade where those new flats are on the corner – that used to be the Bristol Manufacturing – and then the flesh was made into gelatine for jellies, the bones were melted down for glue and all that sort of thing and in those days all the hair would be used for cushions or chairs or even beds. There was no wastage whatsoever.

The work was hard and demanding:

It was all piece work so it was hard graft. If you got to [be] the foreman, no, but for everybody else yes! We used to start early about seven o'clock when I first started, it went on to about half past seven – summat like that and you'd put a full day in. The hooter would go and you'd start work. The hooter was situated somewhere just outside the office and if you was right down by the tan yard you couldn't hear anything else because the drums would be going what they drummed the shoulders in and loads of mechanical machines, huge machines working so you wouldn't have heard without that going. Eventually that stopped after a while because with the foreman on each floor you knew when it was time to start work anyway and as soon as you got in you was on piece work so you didn't need telling that the more you could do the more money you earned!

I had boots with hobnails in, I used to wear leggings right up to here like this, done up, and they'd be as stiff as boards. You never wore anything decent because funnily enough winter or summer you didn't really feel the cold whatever 'cos you was on the go all the time. There was no heating, only upstairs.

What you got to remember is that in the lime yard and the tanning, you used to have to walk on a nine inch [wide brick wall] round all the pits, pulling hides over. It was precarious but the point was you got so used to it it was so natural. I fell in a lime pit and I fell in a tan pit but practically everybody who worked there ended up falling in one time or another. Some of them's about 12 foot deep and anybody that tells you they've never fell in, that's a lie, right! They got to get you out really quick if you fall in the lime pit obviously but there's always somebody there, you know your mate. You used to have to use hooks and they were suspended on a cradle so as it was moving all the time. Then you'd unhook it and then you'd have to pull the hide from pit to pit and do that all through the processes.

Basically that's it without going into everything. Yes they were all indoors, it was all under cover. The only part like you had the 'dock' as we called it the outside part, which is still there now. It looks a bit in disrepair now, the tan yard. You can see it from the opposite side of the road, from the old tobacco warehouses.

From time to time, the pits in which the hides were limed and tanned had to be cleaned out:

I think the worst part of the job was when you had to clean them out because of the liquid. The lime yard not so bad, but even in the lime yard, once you finished with a pit of lime that had been the last processed, they'd drain the pit out and you'd have sediment in it thick like jelly. That would be hosed down so you had to get in the pit with a hose and hose it down.

When David lived with his mother and grandmother in a house on Exeter Road, the various family cats originated in the tannery:

The biggest problem was getting them 'cos we kept wild cats [there]. They used to sleep in the back of the boiler house and you couldn't get near them hardly. They were wild cats, but when they had kittens Albert Clapp who worked there, he used to put on great big gloves and he'd go in and grab the kittens. Beautiful cats. We had beautiful cats and I mean you could domesticate them when they was old enough. The cats, they was real killers – well they were there for a reason. I used to have to go out on the 'dock' at night with me father and we'd walk round with two big lights. When it was closed, that was part of our job, 'cos we lived in those houses [refers to the pair of cottages on Clift House Road] and we had to walk round the 'docks' just to make sure everything was alright, walk all the way down the side of the tan house. You'd walk round the 'docks' and you'd hear this scudding and you'd turn the torch round. Oh God – bloody rats! They was massive. They was as big as the cats, but the cats, they'd tear them apart. It's the only way you could keep them down 'cos at the bottom of the 'dock' where you took all your waste and all that the chute used to come out for everything into the [New] Cut. It was horrible.

David remembers others who worked in the tannery at the same time, including a few women – in spite of the long hours and physical nature of the work:

We had one – Mavis. She worked on the rounding table and she was like a bloke 'cos I must admit after you worked there for a few years you was as strong as a bloody [–]. Did anybody say to you about Popes that used to live in Lime Road? Father and son. Pope the son would be roughly my age now, but he went in there about two years before I left and he was still in there right up to retirement. I used to work with his father in the lime yard because although they had hard jobs, Bill Pope – every night he'd go home and have his tea in Lime Road and he'd walk down the road to the Coopers Arms, nearly every night, and his mate Jack Bath. Yeah, he was a funny little chap. He lived up in Knowle West, he wasn't very tall and he used to have to do what they call scudding and they'd have to lean over an oval shaped thing, a scudder in their hands, a blade, and they'd turn the hide over and scud off all the excess flesh that was left on clean them off. They had a hard job bending over there every day but they was as hard as nails. 'Cos what you got to remember is when I went in there we had about three Polish blokes working for us. We had a Polish woman – she worked upstairs in the drying rooms. We had a few foreigners but the Polish blokes that worked for us they put them mostly in the lime yard and tan yard and they was as strong as bloody horses. They didn't mind piece work but they was all alright, you had your laugh and joking whatever but there was no sort of animosity because of who you was, you know what I mean. Didn't matter about nationality. We had a German – alright, somebody might have called him a kraut in the heat of the moment, in an argument, but there was no animosity. It was all forgotten, but yeah it was alright, no trouble. I worked with a man called Cliff Workman come the end and we used to operate the striking machine right up the top of the factory striking buttons. It was a lovely atmosphere 'cos like I say, it was like one big family so you knew everybody. Old Mr Brierley, he was alright. He'd always speak to you – say good morning, whatever. No, not every day, but he'd come in pretty regular but he'd always come in his Rolls Royce. He had a beautiful Rolls Royce and park him outside the office block. I'll give him his due – he was a gentleman.

David went to work at the tannery in 1952 when he was 15 and during his time there 'went from the lime yard and worked right the way through the whole factory until I ended up on the top floor on the striker.' He earned £22-a-week doing piece-work which was a good wage at the time. Because of his experience, he was confident of taking over from his father as foreman when he finished work, but the new managers had other plans and asked David to train a complete newcomer instead:

> They brought this bloke down from [another] factory and to be honest with you he didn't know one end of a cow from another and I was damned if I was gonna do six months bloody training with him and end up back on the shop floor and he had the job! They came up the next day – begged me to come back but I said no and just packed it in.

Within three days of leaving the tannery, David Ridley got a job with WD&HO Wills where he worked for the next 23 years.

The land owned by the tannery company extends along Clift House Road as far as the large red brick warehouse (C Bond), at one time providing space for allotments which were allocated to some of the employees. The families of both Brenda Hatter and David Ridley grew vegetables there in the 1920s and '30s:

> As you go along Clift House Road on the right hand side, you see a set of gates there and there's a building behind it. Well that building wasn't there years ago. That used to be other allotments inside that wall. My dad had one and then we had one down the back. Where that red brick wall thing is used to be a huge greenhouse on one side and the rest was allotments. (David Ridley)

> My parents had an allotment which is now the Riverside Garden Centre back of the bonded warehouse. You went through a gate and there were quite a few

allotments there. There could have been about eight there on that one plot and then you went further along where my grandfather had one there could have been about the same number there. I can remember going there right till – I'm not sure when it was it closed down and they were offered plots down part of the Ashton Court Estate. My parents liked their allotment. My mother would spend all day on her allotment and it was a nice thing I always liked it as well. I've got pictures of me in my pram at the allotment. (Brenda Hatter)

Working at Wills

In its heyday, the giant Wills Factory No.3 on Raleigh Road employed thousands of people who, in the main, lived close by. Barbara Hickery remembers 'their green overalls being absolutely smothered in smoke.' Dorothy Pike's mother was one of the Wills' Girls:

A lot of my school friends went to Wills, any amount, particularly those who belonged to the church. Naturally then the church was the focal point. If you wanted any 'dos' of any description you always went to the church. And most of them worked there. My mother worked there as a matter of fact. She was one of the first to ever go there, when they opened.

Alma Chalmers' mother also worked there:

Mum had to work in the cigarette factory during the war. You had to go to work – married women had to work – and she was sent there. She hated every minute of it. She used to talk about 'stripping' the tobacco, which she couldn't do quickly enough and [as] they were on piece work, the girls didn't like it much because she [held them up].

When he went to work in the Bedminster Wills factory, David Ridley found himself earning considerably less than he had received round the corner at the tannery. However, he quickly established a new work routine which helped to make up the shortfall:

Well, I went into Wills for £11 3s 9d so I had half me money and I already had four children and a mortgage, so it was a bit of – you know. But the point was, I went into Wills and at the time I was lucky because In those days everybody smoked and then they brought in all the Embassy fags and once they brought in them it just took off. So my money went back up. I could do piece-work on assembling. I could work two hours a day overtime and at weekends, so after about six months things more or less went back to normal, plus the fact I was going to get a pension and all the rest of it. I had a brown coat on – within two years I was training, and within three years I was the first stage of supervision like – a stand-in – and then after eight years I became a supervisor. I ended up, I was assistant foreman over there 'cos I went right through the warehouse as well. There again, when I went into Wills it was fabulous. The old factories they were like not work places – yeah well it was work places, but you knew everybody who worked there in the warehouse or wherever you worked. Most of my family ended up in Wills. Me brother went into Wills from the tannery, me brother-in-law went into Wills, one of me sons worked for Wills, our Julie worked there for some time and me eldest daughter worked there.

Nowadays, little remains of the once great industrial landscape of this part of Bristol. The site of one of the largest Wills factories, situated on Raleigh Road and demolished in 1992, is now occupied by Amerind Grove care home and Aldi supermarket. Gone, too, is the Sunrise Brewery on North Street, although much of the brick building remains and brewing has recently begun again, albeit on a much smaller scale than was once the case. However, a few prominent industries continue to operate locally – the engineering firms of Braby and Babcock, situated either side of Winterstoke Road, and one of the last traditional tanneries in the country on Clift House Road.

Chapter 6

ENDURING THE WAR

On a Sunday night, father went out to the front door when the bombs were dropping and he said 'It's our turn tonight!'

Sheila Williamson

It was clear from the start of the war that Bristol, along with other major cities, would be a target for German bombers. The suburbs of south Bristol, close to the docks and en route for the aircraft factories at Filton, lay in a direct flight path and barrage balloons appeared in the skies as deterrents to low-flying aircraft. Janet Steel remembers the balloon operated from a position 'by the central bandstand' in Greville Smyth park and Len Hatter recalls one 'on Gores Marsh, at the junction of Winterstoke Road and Smyth Road. The crew used to sit in a cage to wind them up and down 'cos if that cable snapped it would smash them to pieces!' Faced with the threat of bombing, arrangements were made for shelters in the neighbourhood. Several people remember using the nearest bonded warehouse, C Bond on Clift House Road:

> That was apparently very safe because the actual entrance way was almost opposite here and the steps went down like that and they reckoned that the only way you could be hurt, you'd have to get a direct hit between the wall and the ground. Anything on top and it wouldn't come through. (Janet Steel)

They had shelters in this warehouse at the end of the road here. We used to go down, to bunk beds, under there. I used to run up the lane when the siren went. (Dorothy Pike)

Unlike Janet, Dorothy was not so confident about what would happen if the warehouse received a hit:

A lot of us went there, a lot of us. You did feel relatively safe with that lot over you, but of course if that lot fell on you, you'd had your chips hadn't you!

Other large buildings, of which there were many in this part of Bristol, were used as shelters:

Another thing they used to do was run across to Ashton Gate School. Underneath in the basement they had an air raid shelter. They used to run across the yard and down the steps into the basement down below. I used to go there as well, carrying my infant. (Dorothy Pike)

I remember going over to one under the tannery. It's the first time I think I ever wore trousers – I had a pair of my father's trousers on or something and it was a dreadful place. (Sheila Williamson)

We had an Anderson shelter in our garden but at certain times, I don't really know why, we used to have to go to the tannery and I used to go with my mother. We'd take blankets and we'd go over to an air raid shelter actually in the tannery. (Brenda Hatter)

Together with many other local people, my mother and I sheltered under the Wills factory buildings. When I think about it, what a very strange place to seek shelter. (Alma Chalmers)

Alma also remembers trudging to the Clifton Rocks Railway and sheltering in the tunnel. Many people were given sheets of tin and other materials to construct Anderson shelters in their back gardens:

We had an air raid shelter which you got to through the end cupboard – you had the larder and the broom cupboard in the scullery – and they made a hole in the wall of the broom cupboard and had a shelter outside which you used to go through to the shelter – it was one of those with a concrete roof. (Janet Steel)

Peggy Triggle and her sister Sheila recall a particularly bad air raid when it was decided that the neighbours' Anderson shelter would be a useless place to stay:

That particular night, we went over to Mr Tiley's [24 Frayne Road] because we always went over to his shelter. They had a shelter and for some reason or other they asked us to go across. And that particular night, they came in and said to us 'I'm ever so sorry but I'm going to have to move you out. It's far too dangerous to stay here tonight.' He said, 'You must come,' and we said, 'Where are we going?' and we had to go in the park [the shelter in Greville Smyth] and we were there for twelve hours. That was the Good Friday raid. It was terrible and apart from that it was very cold. When we got up in the morning, everything was frozen as well.

The Triggle sisters still clearly remember an air raid shelter in Greville Smyth Park although nowadays nothing remains to mark its existence. The shelter remained in place for some time after the war and according to Lew Pedlar, it was used by local football teams as a changing room. It is possible that the shelter was originally provided for the soldiers manning the barrage balloon in the park, though no one would be turned away in an air raid. In 1940 Hazel Coles was ten when her family moved from Somerset into a house on Ashton Road and were immediately caught up in an air raid:

There was a blitz that night and by the side of us where the City Football Ground was the bus station. We had no idea where the air raid shelters were and we came out and the men who worked in there on nights said, 'Come into our shelter.' They had built a little shelter in there, but when we came out it was by the petrol pumps! The next day dad went and found out where the shelter was – well there was a big underground shelter in Ashton Park, so before we went to bed every night we had to put our clothes on the settee, siren suits for the babies and other things, and rabbit and run over to the shelter. The entrance to the shelter was – they used to have a bandstand in the park and it was where the bandstand was, just down past there to go down under the ground. The vicar from, I think, St Francis used to come and check. He had a list, check we were all in there, all your names you know, everybody here. And then the all clear'd go, and we'd all go back to our homes and sometimes we had to go back again. It was quite a thing.

Whatever forms the shelters took, they are remembered as being uncomfortable places:

But it was a nasty night that was – I can remember it so clearly. My mother was completely terrified down there. Because you needed to go to the loo and you had to get and find a bucket somewhere you know. I mean – my mother was in quite a tizz-was. (Peggy Triggle)

I met somebody years and years after, she said 'Oh I remember you in the shelter – you used to sing 'Jesus Bids us Shine'!' (Dorothy Pike)

For some, the whole experience proved too much:

The funniest thing of all really, I remember was – my grandmother took umbrage. The first time the sirens went, my father put her in the cupboard under the stairs. And my grandmother, she came out from the cupboard, packed her bag and went up to live with my auntie at Filton. (Sheila Williamson)

To escape the bombing, other families resorted to leaving the city altogether either overnight when air raids were expected, or until the war was over:

The bombing was the thing that my dad was worried about. He used to drive out from work and pick us up and we would go down to Tickenham. We would stay overnight – every night – not just weekends, in case of the night raids. Because with my grandfather – you see the air raid shelter was under the bonded warehouse at the top of the road and so for him it was very difficult because he walked very slowly, with a walking stick, and if my father was on Home Guard duty my mum would have had him and me – a little toddler – so they thought it be best if we all stayed down there [Tickenham]. So we used to go out every night and come home the next morning when I would go to school. My dad would go on to work. (Janet Steel)

About 1943–44 there was a bomb fell on the house a couple of doors up and our house was damaged and my mother and I went down to Birtle in Somerset where we had friends, my father didn't come 'cos he still had his warden duty and I stayed there I suppose till the end of the war and came back and by then they'd repaired some of the houses. (Brenda Hatter)

There are even tales of families going to spend the night in fields around Long Ashton during the summer months:

Of course a lot of people from the Ashton area used to go out to Long Ashton during the war, to sleep in the fields to try and get away from Bristol, like, thinking they'd be safer out there than they would in Bristol. (Hazel Coles)

Several bombs fell in the Ashton Gate area, a row of houses in Clift Road receiving a direct hit:

We were bombed completely. We had the honour of the bomb! We were bombed on December 2nd. The biggest raid, when the heart of Bristol went was November 24th. The house [number 15] was knocked out into the middle of the road. I was in my mother's Anderson shelter. When we had the bomb the people next door were under the stairs – the Allens – subsequently they both died. It was shock probably. Number 14, yes. (Dorothy Pike)

There were a couple dropped at the bottom where Mrs Pike lives, in the newer houses [part of the terrace which was bombed and the houses replaced with ones of similar design]. And over the far side, there was a bomb dropped there that night. That was a very bad night, the houses were just destroyed. They picked all the bricks up and took them away and just left it until after the war as an empty space. (Peggy Triggle and Sheila Williamson)

The same bomb caused severe damage to the backs of nearby houses on Frayne Road. Janet Steel clearly remembers returning to the family home – number 12:

> My mother walked up and opened the front door and she said, 'Good Heavens above! Whatever's happened here?' And in the porchway, all the glass from the inner door was all over the lobby. So she stepped back out and she went to the front window because we used to have these boards that fitted in for the blackout and everything, and there was no glass in the windows. And she went back and she said to me, 'You stay there – and don't touch anything!' And she went through and she came back out again and said, 'Oh dear. We better get your father home from work.' And luckily we had a telephone so she went through to the middle room and said to my dad, 'You'd better come back home. The back of the house has gone!'

In one raid, the car belonging to the local doctor was lifted into the air by the bomb blast and according to David Ridley, landed on top of the nearby pub:

> It blew up off the road like, where the doorway is, and it finished up on the Hen and Chicken! It was still there when the war finished. They 'ad quite a bit of damage in Greville Road. Two or three places got it.

Alma Chalmers is sure that there was a surgery in Greville Road, near the pub, and the doctor lived in rooms above. Even though he was only five at the time, David Ridley, who was living with his family in Exeter Road, remembers the raid well:

> My brother slept in the back bedroom and the masonry off the roof and the granite blocks came over [from the houses in Greville Road] and went right through the back bedroom ceiling and took the bed and legs right through the floor so they was sticking out in the kitchen. Luckily he wasn't in bed and I was over the air raid shelter when they dropped, but it 'it me off – I was on the top bunk and went straight up on the metal thing 'cos it was such a vibration!

According to David Ridley whose father was working there throughout the war, the tannery on Clift House Road escaped being bombed, in spite of occupying a prominent site close to the docks:

> No I don't think the tannery was hit at all. My dad was in there all those years and he never come home and said [anything about bomb damage].

Several people have vivid memories of seeing the docks and the centre of Bristol being bombed:

> When the 'all clear' went, we all got out and walked up Coronation Road, not knowing that there were, in fact, unexploded bombs there. We walked all the way up Coronation Road because the wood yard, the other side of Vauxhall Bridge, was all ablaze. The wood was all ablaze. You can imagine what it was like – all that wood the burning. We sat and watched it and it wasn't until we got back home and were told off by the police who said, 'You had no business to be going!' Sheila Williamson

Janet Steel was on her way back from visiting relatives in Tickenham:

> We actually were coming home the night of the first big blitz in Bristol. I have very few recollections of the war, but I do remember this vividly. And we're coming across the high road from Tickenham, the Failand Road, and we're just near the golf course and my father said, 'Whatever's happening?' Bristol was lit up, was just lit up with flares and my grandfather was sitting in the back with me and he said, 'Good Lord! Whatever is it?' And my dad said, 'Well, I don't know what it is, but I'm not going on any further.' And he turned around in the entranceway of the golf club and we went back to Tickenham. And so when we came in then next day, we found there had been this dreadful raid. It was the one where they just chucked everything at Bristol and lit the place up. It was – the flares and everything – it was just like day.

Among the casualties in this part of Bristol was St Francis church in North Street, a magnificent Victorian building made from local bricks.

Alma Chalmers still remembers the aftermath of the direct hit which destroyed it:

A memory that is very clear, even now, is the night that St Francis was bombed. This particular night, it was Wills factory [air raid shelter] for us. After the 'all clear', we were walking back home along Greenway Bush Lane and there, in front of us, was St Francis Church ablaze. I clapped my hands together and said to mum how pretty it was. I'm not sure whether I had a quick clip around the ears or a very stern telling off, but I do remember now that my poor mum cried all the way home. I shall never ever forget it. But I can see how pretty it looked to a child.

After one heavy raid, Peggy Triggle remembers looking across the Cut and watching all the timber yards burning on Baltic Wharf: 'The whole city was ablaze. It was a dreadful sight that was.'
As food was rationed in the shops, people found other ways of providing their own:

When everything was in short supply, some people kept chickens. One afternoon a lady I knew well gave me an egg, telling me to take it home to mum and I could have boiled egg for tea, but to be very careful with it. I was very careful and kept squeezing it to see if it was still there! Yes – you're right – I squeezed too hard and it broke in my Sunday school best coat pocket! Egg everywhere but no boiled egg for tea, and more washing for mum. (Alma Chalmers)

In common with most public spaces, Greville Smyth Park was given over to families in the neighbourhood so that they could grow vegetables:

There were railings all round the park [and] they cut those down for the war effort. And they had allotments in the park. Nice allotments, very nice they were. (Dorothy Pike)

One family which grew their own produce were the Shorts:

Living in Clift House Road, we were able to rent an allotment on the site which is now Riverside Nursery. My husband loved gardening and grew lots of fruit and vegetables. Behind the allotment was the bonded warehouse where, in the last years of the war, I would run to the shelter with my baby daughter in my arms, complete with gas mask etc! (Thelma Short)

Many local people were quickly caught up in what became known as 'the war effort'. Mervyn Southway vividly remembers his time in the army:

I went into the army in May 1943. I was actually on the Battle of Britain. I was on radar. We were in London, after I had gone through all the passing of the tests and everything, a three months' course and all that – or a six weeks' course. So we were in London at the time and then of course the raids started and the equipment that we had was pahh! – rubbish! Well the flying bombs and planes – in actual fact, they used to fire the guns over the tops of the houses – no hope of hitting the plane. For the morale of the people, they were doing something! Then the flying bombs started so we moved down to the coast, all the battery – that's the guns and everything. They were coming across, yes they were coming across. Of course we had different equipment: it was an American radar which was very much more accurate and they used shells that apparently they were supposed to have been naval shells and they told us you had to be careful how you handled them because they could explode! And where they had them stacked they had a guard on them every night. We all did guards on it, you know. So of course that was the thing – and when the shell got to within, I think it was 50 feet of the object, it would explode so they couldn't fire them on a cloudy day 'cos the flying bomb would be above the clouds and the bomb would explode when it got to within 50 feet of the cloud. We had our fighter planes out over the sea and then we were the next with the radar and all the equipment – the predictor and all the rest of it – and then beyond that was the balloon barrage. We went on the course, you see, near Reading it was – we went on the course, I think it was six weeks – and I mean, for what we learned...well...but you pick it up as you go along. And with this other radar which was an American one, 'cos the Americans come in very late and that was it – we used that and eventually the flying bombs died out. I mean, we knew when a flying bomb left, over the other side, over in France, but the Secret Service had informed everyone over here, they'll be over at twelve o'clock and sure enough the first one came over!

All men who were too old to serve in the Forces, but who were fit enough for duty like Brenda Hatter's father, were drafted into local service. Brenda remembers helping him out:

> He was a kind of warden. I don't know if he was an ARP warden or what and sometimes he had to check on people in the different houses in our section of Coronation Road which went up to Greenbank Road and he gave me the job, we had a big ledger book and I used to go to all the houses and get them to sign the ledger book so he knew the people were still the occupiers of that house.

Dorothy Pike's husband 'couldn't go into the army because he had bad eyesight and so of course he was a warden. You had to do something.' Janet Steel's father 'was in the Home Guard, which was down on Duckmoor Road.'

As part of the build-up to D-Day, American troops were stationed around Bristol:

> Of course when the Americans came they had all the chewing gum and all the sweets and we never had it because of course we never had the coupons to go and get sweets and things in them days. And of course all the children, they used to go along and if they spoke to these Americans, they p'raps give them a chewing gum or a sweet you know and all that. In fact there was one American, he was a very nice man and when our children was over in the park, he'd sit down and talk to them and then he wanted to know a bit about Bristol and they'd try and tell 'im you know. And then he came and seen my mum and he said, 'Would you mind if I took your children out? I'd like to see the Suspension Bridge.' And mum said, 'Well I'm very funny. I'm an old-fashioned mother and I like my children to be home.' Anyway, he said 'Well you know I'll bring them home, at a certain time' and all this. Anyway, they took him down to Hotwells so that he could look up and see the Suspension Bridge. Along the Cut they went, took him different places, and he was quite impressed with it all. And he was very, very kind and he knocked on the door one day and he gave mum a big bag of sweets and he said, 'Thank you very, very much.' He was a nice man you know. (Hazel Coles)

Once the remains of ruined buildings had been cleared and the area made safe, bombsites provided wonderful opportunities for children's games:

Now, the bombed buildings were famous! That was the most wonderful play area in the whole – it was even better than Ashton Park! Well – it was a lovely flat area. They cleared it, took everything off it so there weren't bits [of debris]. It was a lovely flat area. So, Bonfire Night – what a wonderful place to have a bonfire! It was big! It was four at least, it could have been five houses that went there, so you had this wonderful area so you used to have your bonfire there. So, air raid shelters. Right, once they were left, they didn't have a doorway or anything, they were just left, so we used to...well all the kids would toddle up North Street and just down opposite, I suppose opposite Ashton Gate School a little road goes down, there was a timber merchant down there, so we used to cadge all the bark strippings off the trees and drag all these bark strippings back home and put them in the air raid shelter you see, until you got nearer Bonfire Night and then you put them out, and then all the kids from Walter Street and Greenway Bush Lane used to come over and pinch our timber, so that's why it was put in the air raid shelter, where they wouldn't see it. So yes, that's where you had your bonfire and all the rest of it. (Janet Steel)

Alma Chalmers and her friends also used a bombsite near their homes for lighting bonfires:

There's a road off of Walter Street called Gilbert Street and a bomb destroyed some of the houses there and we used to spend hours playing on that bombsite. The thing I can remember the most is the terrible smell. Whether it was the burning or the remains of the burning, it was a terrible, terrible smell, and from that day on, we always had our Bonfire Night bonfire there, on that site.

Janet Steel recalls other games:

And also we used to, again go round to Twogood's I think it was, the timber yard, and cadge some more of this bark and the older boys made a den, a house, on this bombed building and it was really smart – all done with bark on the outside, you know and it had a counter. Then we used to cadge at home. Everybody would go home and see what was going: 'Has your mother got anything left that we could cook?' So we used to cook – we used to shovel it all in a saucepan and boil it up together and I used to get some of my mother's curry powder and potatoes and cabbage and carrot and whatever. We're talking about when I was eleven – about '47, '48 – that sort of time. And this is in the school holidays. And so we'd make these wonderful stews and then the older ones would go in behind the counter and you'd have to queue up with your plate at the counter – because we'd built a counter – and you'd get stew. That was your dinner. We had wonderful times over there, on the bombed buildings! So that was the hub of the thing.

Sheila Hall remembers similar imaginative play taking place on the bombsites:

> When I was a little girl, I used to play on the bombsite near us. We used to build houses out of bricks and get some jam jars and weeds for your flowers, put stones in for your sweets and things to sell in your 'shop'.

There were a number of prisoner-of-war (POW) camps in this part of Bristol although their exact location is subject to a certain amount of speculation. Dorothy Pike recalls the nearest camp:

> If you go over to the avenue, which was Ashton Avenue, there used to be prisoners-of-war there. There was a camp there.

Other people also recall POW camps in a similar location:

> They had the prisoner camps in Ashton. They called it the Black Hills when we were young you know. There was the bus station and go round the corner and Braby's the steel works was there and then you go across the road and I think there's a public house there, by the railway line. You go across there and that's where well, they had the prisoners there I know, German prisoners. (Hazel Coles)

> I can remember during the war along the long road which goes from where the swing bridge used to be to the motor works, on that side used to be a camp, a

prisoner-of-war camp or an American camp I can't remember. There were several camps. There was another off the Whitening Yard, just the other side of the railway line. (Brenda Hatter)

When he was nine or ten years old, Lew Pedler would explore the disused POW camp 'which was called White City':

There was another prisoner-of-war camp on the site where Strachan and Henshaw [now Babcock] is that's called the Whitening Yard. Although I can't remember the actual camp itself, the Americans were running that site and they left behind quite a lot of armour gear – cars, jeeps etc – and we used to have a wonderful time imagining what they were doing with those jeeps. They left them there quite a long time before they started clearing them out and developing the site.

Hazel Coles also remembers people making cakes as treats for the British troops who had been held prisoner on their return home:

Mrs Williams, my mum's friend, put an advert – I can't remember if it was in a paper. I think it must have been in the *Evening Post* or, if it wasn't the *Evening Post* it was the *Evening World* or something then – saying when the soldiers came home, Mrs Williams said if they provided, of course it was on rations, provided the goods, she'd make a cake. And she did. She used to make cakes for them, when they came home, to welcome them. My uncle he was a prisoner in the Italian and German hands and he came home and he came to see us and I remember Mrs Williams made a lovely cake for him.

Once it was clear that the war was coming to an end, the task of rebuilding damaged and destroyed properties got underway:

Our house was rebuilt because it was only the very back. They actually did that while the war was still on. But we didn't have the garden walls. [They] weren't built properly. We moved back for the end of the war. We still had a couple of little trips to the air raid shelter but not that many. At that time, I was that little bit older and we thoroughly enjoyed ourselves. We had great fun – probably drove all the people round here mad! (Janet Steel)

We were very foolish when we were bombed, because a lot of people had nothing but a soap box, and claimed – you had to put a claim in. Of course you only got what you claimed for. Some people got a new home for nothing, but I'm afraid we lost most of ours. In fact we lost everything. You don't think how much a cup and saucer costs, do you? You don't put that down. Everything went. We lost absolutely everything. Well, I say everything: I think there's a cupboard in the other room which was saved. No, we had one chair I think it was. Before I was married I made a collection of cut glass for the bedroom. I lost every stitch of everything I had, all my tumblers, everything went. Well, we had the direct hit so there you are. We had a very, very nice grate in the front room, and one of the neighbours saw somebody taking the grate out one night and carrying it back – they lived up in Coronation Road – the end of my grate! Not that I wanted it, but I'd rather they'd said we would like it, rather than come and take it. I used to come down and have a look and see what they were doing you know. It was Mrs Heard who lived next door but one, she was instrumental in getting Weeks to rebuild it, because I was all for Stones. They did give us the option. I know she got in touch with Weeks. It was very good anyway. And of course all the doors are nice because they weren't bombed and we had all their seasoned timber. Their timber was well seasoned because they hadn't used it during the war. (Dorothy Pike)

Although several people remember wartime casualties, we do not know exactly how many people living in this part of Bristol were killed or injured during the bombing raids. The relief when the war ended was immense and very apparent, judging by the memories of the various celebrations which took place:

We lived in Coronation Road when the war ended and they had VE and VJ they called it, and all the people in like Walter Street and Mary Street, Peter Street and that, they all got together and we went. I remember my sister and me, and I think my big brother, and they all had saucepans, tin tubs, oh they had everything you could think that made a noise, trumpets, whistles and we marched! I can't

The Victory Tea Party, 1945 or 46, at which, as Brenda Hatter says, 'We all dressed up'. Brenda Hatter (née Baylis) is on the far right, with the Union Jack. The picture was taken in Ashton Gate Road.

Taken on the same day, now ready for tea, local people give the victory salute. Brenda is the third child back diagonally from the left corner of the front table, still in Union Jack costume. Both of these pictures were taken by A. Scoins, Photographer, 32 Lime Road, BS3.

remember which way we went, whether we went up along Coronation Road like up to Bedminster Bridge or whether we went down Hotwells. I can remember we came back along Coronation Road but I can't remember how we went and we were banging these things and my mum she gave my sister a saucepan, and I think I had a saucepan and, well by the time we came back, the tin tubs and the saucepans was nearly right through where they banged and they shouted – and the noise! And then they had street parties, and though we lived in Coronation Road, we were invited to Walter Street and I think it was Mary Street 'cos they had big bonfires in the middle of the roads and we was all dancing, all round the bonfires and they had children's parties and we were invited to go down to there 'cos all our friends lived down there. My grandmother, she come from the country so she didn't know nothing about all this, so I said 'Come on gran, I'll take you down to the fire. Come and see 'em all dancing.' So what did I do – went in the front room and got mum's fur coat and put that on 'cos it was cold, and went down to the fire and in the end my gran and I were dancing round the fire and I had mum's fur coat on! Oh gosh, when I think about it. (Hazel Coles)

We were going to make flags you see, to go across the road in Walter Street. We've got the Union Jack and we've got this that and the other, but we haven't got a Russian flag you see and it was most important that we had a Russian flag. So my dad is going to paint it on a sheet, this flag, this Russian flag. He's got the kitchen table and he's painting the sickle and whatever, you know, and an old aunt comes to see us while we're doing this, and she's about this wide and she wears bloomers like, as big as you can imagine! And she sits on the table when he's finished his flag to get this sickle on her bum! So she went home with the hammer and sickle – she did it deliberately! We were all on a high, everyone's on a high 'cos the war's ended you know. So she goes home with this sickle on her bloomers! (Alma Chalmers)

Chapter 7

SCHOOL DAYS

Sitting in Ashton Gate Primary School on a hot sunny afternoon with the windows open, you very clearly heard 'Worker's Playtime' coming from the Wills factory. I think it was regular round about 2.30–3.45 in the afternoon and you would be doing your work and you could hear it very clearly because they broadcast it throughout the whole factory.

Stephen Williamson

The Ashton Gate area is well served by schools, with Ashton Gate Primary School and Ashton Park School close at hand. Inevitably, various changes have taken place over the years to the schools in this part of Bristol, as Stephen Williamson describes. His father, Dick Williamson, taught locally and worked in the school on all these sites:

The present Ashton Gate Primary School was originally two schools, Ashton Gate Junior and Southville Secondary Modern for Boys. I attended Ashton Gate Junior School from 1955 to 1962, throughout which time the buildings on the corner of North Street and Greenway Bush Lane and the large playground behind formed the Secondary Modern School – Ashton Gate Juniors being accessed from two entrances on Ashton Gate Terrace. Southville Secondary Modern School also had an annexe in Raynes Road.

In 1963, Southville Secondary Modern for Boys was merged with the equivalent school for girls, situated in Beauley Road, the site now occupied by the Southville

Centre. At this point, the Greenway Bush Lane premises became part of Ashton Gate Junior School and the new Southville Secondary School, catering for both boys and girls, occupied the Beauley Road site. The Raynes Road annexe was closed as a school at this point.

In the late 1960s or early '70s, Southville Secondary was amalgamated with Ashton Park Secondary School to create a large comprehensive school serving this part of Bristol. The Beauley Road site was used until sometime in the mid-1980s as Ashton Park Lower School, housing the first and second years – Years 7 and 8 as they are today.

Jantzen Derrick's school experience in the 1940s confirms the names of the various schools as they were at that time:

I went to Ashton Gate Primary School which is in the same situation now, even though they've enlarged the school because Ashton Gate Primary School and Southville Secondary Modern School were together there and the smaller part was the primary school and the larger part was the senior school. You spent the first couple of years there, at Southville, and then they had an annexe round the back of the football ground.

It was prefabricated buildings and for the last two or three years of your school you went there. That was called Raynes Road School and I was there until I left school at 15.

A similar pattern of schooling was also followed by David Ridley, although he began his education at Southville Primary on Stackpool Road:

I moved from Southville Juniors down to Ashton Gate [Primary] and then when I was 11, we moved into the prefabricated school at the end of Raynes Road where the City ground car park is. It was all prefabricated buildings. I went there till I was 15 and I ended up, I think for the last six months, over to Ashton [Park] School in Lady Smyth's [Ashton Court Park]. You know the school in Lady Smyth's: all my children went there.

Starting school is a memorable experience for most people. Lew Pedler not only recalls the names of his first teachers, but also what he wore on his first day:

Off I went to school at Ashton Gate, into the nursery department, and my badge was a ship or a yacht, a little blue smock with the ship as the marker. We had basically lessons and playtime all through the morning. Miss Brookman and Miss Perryman were the two teachers at the time. I remember we used to have to go to sleep in the afternoon on folding camp beds with just a piece of canvas across them. All the tables and chairs got moved out of the way and the camp beds were put out and we had an hour's kip. (Lew Pedler)

Lew remembers the headmistress at that time (c1948) was Miss Edbrook who was followed by Miss Jones.

Brenda Hatter, who began school at Ashton Gate Primary in 1939 when she was four, also recalls having an afternoon sleep:

We used to have to go to bed on little small camp beds. I can't remember much about the teachers, I remember some of the teachers but not many of them by their names. I enjoyed school and I was there until I was 11. I left Ashton Gate and I went to Southville School in Beauley Road for a short time. I took the Bristol Commercial Exam to pass to go to Commercial School. Unfortunately I failed and my parents decided to send me to Clark's College which I went to from when I was about 12 'til I was about 15. That was a commercial college where I learnt mainly book-keeping, typing and shorthand.

Not every child was happy about having to go to school. Hazel Coles describes what happened when one of her younger sisters, Georgina, was taken to Ashton Gate for the first time:

She went in and sat on a little seat. She went in lovely, all excited, and then a couple of days after, my mum was home and the back door went – 'cos we could keep our doors open then – and Georgina [had] come home from school. She said, 'I've had enough. I've been to school long enough so I've come home.' She was five! My mum said, 'Oh no, you've got to stay in school' and she got ready and took her back down to school again and told the teacher [that] she'd come home.

Hazel's brothers attended Southville Secondary School where the pupils were encouraged to take part in a weekly raffle, which one of the brothers won on a regular basis, much to his mother's despair:

I don't know what it was [for but] they used to have chinchilla rabbits [as prizes] and I think we had more rabbits than anybody else. 'Cos every time, he used to win the rabbit! Oh my mum – she used to dread Fridays. She used to say, 'He's took his money for a raffle. I bet we'll have another rabbit!' Dear, dear, dear – we had all these different rabbits.

Although it meant further to travel from her home in Frayne Road, Janet Steel's parents chose a school away from the immediate area:

I started school when I was four and I went to a little private school in Acramans Road which was just behind St Paul's Church and it was run by a Miss Berryman – Adelina M Berryman!

Like so many children of her generation, Janet's education was disrupted by the war, her family moving to Tickenham to escape the bombing and Janet having to attend school in Clevedon.

Teachers are remembered with a mixture of fondness, reverence – as well as a certain degree of fear, even after many years:

I eventually ended up with Miss Mountain and I think that was the only time in my scholastic career that I was ever top of the class. I've still got my reports from Ashton Gate School. Then afterwards I went into Mr Jones's class who was still there up until the last 15 years or so 'cos my own children went to Ashton Gate School and Glyn Jones was the only permanent feature there. I went into Mr Wright's class [next]. [He] didn't have a classroom in the main school. In Ashton Gate Road on the opposite side of Greenbank Road was a church and church hall and they used to have a class there and I was in there with Mr Wright. I can remember

Glyn Jones and Jeff Wright, when the staff [put on an entertainment] for the kids, actually doing a duet – Glyn on the piano and Jeff on the clarinet. Yes the staff performed for the kids. After Mr Wright, I spent two years with Miss Challenger. In a sense I was a bit unlucky I suppose because Norah Challenger and indeed Olga Mountain, were also members of St Paul's Church, Bedminster which my parents were members of and Norah Challenger was a contemporary of my mother. They were in the bible class together so when I went into Norah Challenger's class there was a little bit of 'I know your mother' and I probably reacted to that because I thought 'No, I don't want to know about this!' My mother had high expectations and when I didn't deliver it was always going to be my fault because there was no way she was going to fall out with her friend Norah Challenger. She was a very fine teacher. Miss Knight was another teacher, very academic but she chose education within the primary sector although she did move over to Ashton Park School when Ashton Park opened. (Lew Pedler)

Another person who remembers being in Miss Challenger's class is Stephen Williamson:

Stephen Williamson with his aunt Margaret Triggle. Taken in Stephen's back garden at 32 Clift Road around 1955. Stephen writes, 'Another try-out for a school uniform. This was for Ashton Gate school, which I attended from 1955-62'.

Oh Miss Challenger – she was a very memorable teacher! The fact that my father was a teacher and in the very late fifties and early sixties taught at Southville Secondary School which is now part of Ashton Gate School, he knew all my teachers and I couldn't breathe out of place without it being reported! Miss Challenger, whose class I was in for my last two years, was an excellent teacher. I couldn't fault her. She used to come to evensong on a Sunday night at St Paul's Church and if I'd done anything wrong I'm sure it was passed on to mum and dad. She was never hesitant in putting the ruler across my knees for kneeling on the chair. I didn't very often sit on the chair, I used to kneel on it and that wasn't acceptable in those days and [so] there was often a red mark at the back of my legs where the ruler was put but it did me no harm.

David Ridley also recalls some of the teachers who taught him, vividly describing the severity of the discipline in schools in the 1940s and '50s:

Ashton Gate [Primary School] – we had a woodwork teacher who was called Johnson, who you didn't muck about with. We had a maths teacher – an arithmetic teacher they was called in them days – called Maddocks. You didn't muck about with him, because years ago if you done summat wrong then you'd have to go out the front and you'd either get the cane, the slipper or the ruler. They were very obliging 'cos you could pick which instrument you wanted! But the only trouble was in those days if you ended up getting the cane across your backside or whatever or the ruler across your hand, my father if he found out you had it at school he used to give me another clout round the ear 'ole at home. Never done any of us any harm.

Anyone who knows the site occupied by Ashton Gate Primary School will be familiar with the playground which is sandwiched between the two main buildings. Lew Pedler has happy memories of playing cricket there:

We also used to play cricket in the playground with the teachers. We used to break windows quite a lot! The caretaker's workshop was in the corner so that used to get bombarded now and again, but you were never encouraged to hit the ball hard anyway – basically defend your wicket and people that could defend their wicket were always going to be in the school team. I was never a core member of the [football] team but I did actually play a few matches for Ashton Gate School when there was a local league. I was the scorer for the cricket team and I scored at least a couple of years.

Ashton Gate Primary School, on its cramped site and with limited playground space, used Greville Smyth Park for various outdoor events like sports days, as Stephen Williamson confirms from his time at the school. The pupils were also taken over to use the pitches on The Clanage in Clanage Road, Bower Ashton.

Another event which Stephen recalls is the opening of St Francis's Church on North Street, following its rebuilding after the war:

> Very soon after it opened, as a school we went over. I can remember we had to learn 'The Lord is my Shepherd' – all six verses. You had to learn them. You couldn't get away and pretend you were singing, not with Miss Challenger and Mr Jones. Yes we learnt that for a service over there. That was the church that the school used for the odd festival.

Few people will deny that school dinners have improved considerably over the years, with a current focus on 'healthy eating'. As a child, Lew Pedler had a particular aversion to meals at school:

Stephen Williamson, August 1962, aged 11, just inside Greville Smyth Park. Stephen recalls: 'This was the first 'outing' in my new school uniform. Shorts were worn well into the second year at school. All items had been purchased from Stephens, the Bristol Cathedral School outfitters, who had a shop in Park Street. The school cap in my right hand I still have today, and it was worn at school until I was 18.'

Brenda Hatter's class at Ashton Gate School in about 1941. Brenda can still remember many of her class-mates names. Brenda is in the middle row second from the left, in the striped dress. Other children include, left to right:
Back row: Geoffrey Symons, John Wedlock, ?, Gordon Whitaker Michael Fowler ?, ?, ?, John Chenowith
Middle row: Ann Delany, Brenda Hatter, Pat Arnold, Pamela Smith, Paul Delany, Pat Crocombe ?, ?, ?, Dorothy Williams
Front Row: ?, ?, Pamela Lane, Graham England,?, ?, Ann Jenkins

...primarily because one school dinner which I hated was on a Friday – boiled fish and peas. They were disgusting! I appealed to my mother and probably broke down in tears [so] it was decided that the best thing I could do was to go home for dinner. The problem was that my mother was working.

Luckily for Lew, his mother's job only occupied her for three days a week and a solution was found for the other two days:

I used to walk from Ashton Gate School across to the Underfall Yard by Cumberland Road which was where my father worked. My father was a crafty devil because he liked his pint at lunchtime. His working lunchtime was 1 till 2 pm so from 12 till 1, I had to bide my time somehow because he was in the pub at 12 o'clock and by the time I used to get along to the Nova Scotia although I wasn't allowed in the pub. I was allowed to stand in between the two doors and out would come the lemonade. It didn't matter if it was raining, winter or summer, whatever I had on. Two or three days a week I would traipse my way over to there I would come back with father and he would cook me a quick dinner and on Tuesdays we were lucky because that was the day of the cockle man. He was one of the family and he used to drive the delivery van around Hotwells and go into the Nova Scotia. He'd have a pint with father and I'd get a lift home with father so there was actually only one day a week I had to walk home. My father was crafty he knew all the wrinkles and many years later I met the guy who was the publican of the Nova Scotia who remembered my father and he said, 'You were the little lad that used to stand outside.' And I said 'Yes' and he said, 'Your father used to come in every day but there was always a lookout somewhere and somebody would pop in and say "Quick, the foreman's around!" And I used to get your father under the counter and out the living room out of the way'. Once one o'clock arrived we were out the door.

Stephen Williamson sums up what it was like to have particular school friends, only to lose them when moving from one school to another:

Of course you walked to school [as] it was so close anyway and the friendship – we sort of walked together – David Hickery, Stephen Southway, people like that. We would meet up and walk to and from school together but then you moved on to secondary school. David went on to Ashton Park, I went to Bristol Cathedral School [in 1962] and that was the end of our friendship and probably the last time I saw him because you tend to drift apart.

Chapter 8

CHURCH, OUTINGS AND SPECIAL EVENTS

You met Eleanor Roosevelt up the church hall didn't you? Didn't you shake hands?

Bob Pike to his mother, Dorothy

It is well documented that church attendance has declined steadily over the years. At one time the local church was regarded as a focal point in the community and there was a general expectation that children would attend the Sunday School linked to the church where their family worshipped as Kath Winter, who grew up before the war, recalls:

We all went to Sunday School in those days and when you went to work you had to have a character [reference] from the Sunday School even working in the factories. They wouldn't take you if you didn't have a character from the Sunday School. I went to St Michaels and All Angels. Really I was Catholic – well my father was Catholic 'cos he was Irish – but I went to a Catholic school till I was seven. He came over in the 1914 war and my mother met him. I've got a picture and they all had moustaches in those days.

The Williamson family from Clift Road were regular members of the congregation at St Paul's Church, Bedminster and Stephen describes the routine which he and his parents followed every Sunday in the 1950s and '60s:

We went to St Paul's Church. I was in the church choir. Dad joined the choir after me but even before I was in the choir it was a twice a day job. You went to the morning service; you came home. Dad always had a sleep in the afternoon so the house had to be quiet. Not allowed out to play on a Sunday with your friends. Not allowed to ride a bike on a Sunday. I think it was fairly common [and] I certainly wasn't in behind a curtain looking at my mates out playing. I think it was generally assumed that Sunday was a day of rest. Then of course it was back for evensong at 6.30 so again up Coronation Road. By the time you were home from that you were thinking about a glass of milk and off to bed. So weekends were fairly routine. Oh, everything revolved around going to church Sunday morning and Sunday evening. I just never recall it being missed unless we were on holiday or something.

Both St Paul's on Coronation Road and St Francis's Church on North Street were bombed in the war, re-opening again in the mid-fifties following extensive repair and rebuilding. Stephen Williamson recounts the arrangements which were made so that church services could continue in the area for the duration of the war:

I don't know what St Francis did after they were bombed but St Paul's had a church hall called St David's Hall at the end of Raleigh Road. It's now flats, at the bottom of Beauley Road where Beauley Road and Raleigh Road meet; the church hall was at the bottom of there. My mum and dad were married in there so it may be that that was the nearest one because I don't know if St Francis had alternative arrangements. I know they had a church hall up there but whether they held services there I don't know. So the church hall was obviously consecrated or whatever was done to make it a place of worship and that was the church we went to and obviously we moved up to St Paul's when it was re-opened. I would have been christened in St David's at the bottom of Beauley Road. When I say St David's, it was St David's Church Hall but it was part of St Paul's.

As a young woman, Stephen's mother, Sheila, had been a member of St Paul's Church until it was bombed and also recalls St David's Hall being brought into use for church services and other occasions:

I was actually married in St David's because St Paul's had been bombed. St David's was still there and Dick [Sheila's husband] was still in the air force then. And then we saw St Paul's rebuilt – we paid for a brick. You paid for a brick every now and then.

Sheila's sister, Peggy, remembers St David's Hall as it was before the war and how it had served other purposes:

Very often at St David's, before the war, on a Friday night we went down to do a little country dancing. We could walk there, you see, and go down at night with no problem whatsoever.

Like the Williamsons, Lew Pedlar's family also attended St Paul's Church – later switching to St Francis's:

Mother and Father were brought up in St Paul's, technically Mother more so than Father, but although I went to St Paul's until about 1950 I went off to St Francis after that so I was at St Francis for about ten years after that I went back to St Paul's again because that's where Di [Lew's wife] went and her parents went. So that's how that sort of changeover came about.

John Hickery remembers St Francis's Church, or rather the consequences of misbehaving there: 'The vicar, silly fool – making me sit with the girls because I was naughty!'

John's wife, Barbara, came from a family which had long-standing links with the Salvation Army chapel in Dean Lane and John clearly recalls its members visiting Clift Road where he grew up: 'They used to get in the street here on a Sunday morning.' Barbara describes a typical Sunday when she was a child growing up in the 1950s:

All our family was Salvationists. I used to go round the streets. Yeah, they used to come round on a Sunday morning [to] different streets. I've done that with my aunties. My aunties and some of my cousins, when they all wore uniforms. They were strong Salvationists. I had to go twice a day on a Sunday – Sunday School down the Salvation Army – and I wasn't allowed to play out in the street on a Sunday. As far as I could go was to sit on the doorstep.

Dorothy Pike confirms the important role which the church played in the local community, often providing a focus for social events, Sunday School outings in particular:

A lot of my school friends went to Wills, particularly those who belonged to the church. Naturally then the church was the focal point. If you wanted any 'dos' of any description you always went to the church. And most of them worked there. My mother worked there as a matter of fact. She was one of the first to ever go there. Well of course a lot of them belonged to chapel, because there was a chapel at the end there, at the end of Greenway Bush Lane.

In spite of the importance of regular church attendance, going on a Sunday school outing was no excuse for being absent from work, as Alma Chalmers remembers only too well:

We had a Sunday school outing which you did in those days and we were going to Weston [super Mare] so the mums could come too. [My mother] came and we had a nice day. She goes off the next day with her note to the [Wills] factory to say 'I'm very sorry it was my daughter's Sunday School outing and I went with her.' They called her in and said, 'Look, we'll give you this back, and if you can bring us a note which says you were unwell, you were poorly, that will be fine.' [But my mother] said, 'No, I don't tell lies!' And they said, 'Well think about it a little bit – you know, that'll be the end of it if you do that.' But she stood by her guns and she said, 'No, I'll say exactly what I did. I went on a Sunday school outing with my daughter.' She was really hauled over the coals for that as you can imagine!

Ashton Gate Methodist Sunday School
GREENWAY BUSH LANE · BRISTOL 3

1849   1949

CENTENARY YEAR

" And they brought young children to Him . . . and Jesus said . . . for of such is the kingdom of God."
St. Mark, c 10, vv 13 14

SOUVENIR PROGRAMME   PRICE · ONE SHILLING

Alma and her husband Bernard Chalmers were regular attenders of the Methodist Chapel which stood on the corner of Greenway Bush Lane and Ashton Gate

The senior (above) and junior (below) Sunday school classes at Ashton Gate chapel. The pictures were published in a booklet celebrating the centenary of the chapel in 1949. The chapel stood in Greenway Bush Lane on its junction with Ashton Gate Road, on land now used by Ashton Gate School. Some of the names that Alma Chalmers remembers include: Senior Department: N Butler [farthest left in picture]; A Britton [back row sixth from left]; A Payne [back row fifth from right]; A Havvock [third row back, first boy on left]; A Simmons [second row back, first man on left]; L Whitlock [woman next to him]; Miss Salter [second row back sixth from right]; Miss Thorne [woman next to her, fifth from right].

In the junior, primary and beginners' department are: F Walters [back row, first left]; Sheila Simmonds [back row second left]; Ethel Clements [back row fourth from left]; T Field [back row, first right]; Syd Willmot [man standing farthest left in picture]; Syd Allward [man standing next to him]; Rose Britton [woman in front of them seated left]; Muriel Lawrence [standing farthest right in picture]; Lily Britton [standing behind her on the right]; Miss Edith Marchant [in front of them, second row back first right, holding child]; F Field [man in centre of picture second row back].

Terrace. Dorothy Pike recalls 'the chapel' and the rivalry between it and the local Anglican churches for members:

> It's gone now. [It stood] right opposite the school. There used to be great rivalry between the church and the chapel, for members. And when it was the outing we always went to Weston, of course, for the Sunday School outing. You went in an open bus, in a large bus, and they used to see if they could get one more bus than we did. Or the church tried to get one more bus than they did! [The chapel] was a very, very thriving concern.

Outings and trips by train

Family fun and relaxation pre-war often took simple forms. Like nowadays, picnics were a popular way of spending the day together as a family, with nearby Leigh Woods and the Ashton Court estate being favourite venues. Peggy Triggle, who grew up in Clift Road in the 1930s recalls such outings:

> In the summertime, on our Saturdays, a picnic would be prepared and I really can't tell what was in the picnic, but it was nothing for us to walk right down by the side of the river and up Nightingale Valley and have our picnic on what was called 'The Plain'. Yes, that's where we used to go. My grandmother, my grandparents and my auntie Kath who lived in Allington Road with her two sons, she would come down and we'd all go up. Sometimes there was quite a few of us go up, from this road. Or else we'd get to go up to the first field at Ashton. We'd go out there for a picnic. It was cows and all and we used to have a picnic under a tree out there. Or else we'd go on the railway from the little Ashton Junction – yes, for about fourpence, and we'd go down to Portishead and then we'd walk across some fields to a bay wasn't it – Lady Bay was it called? And we'd have a picnic there. Yes – it was such a different world altogether, but a very happy one.

Peggy also remembers the annual family trip to a nearby orchard to collect apples which her mother then stored for winter eating:

> Going back to just before the war, in the autumn, Mum used to go down to right at the end of Bower Ashton. There was an orchard there and this little dotty soul there

sold all the apples, and Mum used to pick out the ones she wanted. She'd buy a whole sack of them and the [owner] used to say, 'I've got special ones for Sheila and Peggy.' It was a special apple and the apple was shaped like a sheep's nose, and she called them 'sheep's noses'! We'd bring them back, then Mum would put all the newspapers and all the apples on top of the wardrobes – that was our last thing we ate at night. She said, 'Go on – one of you go up and get two apples down.' And we'd go up and stand on her chair and get our two apples down and rush down quick because it was dark up there! They would last the winter – they were winter apples. They were such a nice little couple and such a lovely orchard there.

Ashton Gate Station (later renamed Ashton Gate Halt), situated at the point where the Portishead line met the Bristol Harbour Railway, was the nearest station to the Ashton Gate area and several people remember taking trips by train along the Avon Gorge:

I used to go to Portishead with mother when I was a schoolboy and I think it was something like sixpence return for me and mother from Ashton Gate Halt as it was called then. And then you had the one [station] over by the Clanage where the [green foot] bridge goes over the top. I forget the name of that one now. Clifton Bridge, yes, Clifton Bridge. And then it used to go on down – you know, to Pill, Portbury – down to Portishead. (Mervyn Southway)

And the Ashton Gate railway station, that was wonderful. It used to be sixpence to go to Portishead. I did that many, many times – more times than I can remember. That was a great outing. And Severn Beach was another place. (Dorothy Pike)

David Ridley and his friends used to take trips to Portishead and Severn Beach by lorry as well as train:

[I] used to go to Portishead loads of times nearly every Sunday. Used to go along to Portishead and then the other side you had the Severn. Used to go along to Severn Beach. I used to go down there with Charlie James's father. He worked for the petroleum company down by the docks and he had one of these great big lorries with high sides for barrels and he used to come home weekends and make sure his lorry was empty and take all of us, all the kids in the street, and we'd all go down. They had great big tyres and go in the Severn Beach lido. I think that's closed now, we was always told, 'Don't put your feet on the floor' [as] there was always broken glass and god knows what in there. (David Ridley)

By the time that Stephen Williamson was growing up in the 1950s, the Portishead line was in decline. It closed to passenger services in 1964, a victim of Dr Beeching's cuts to the national railway network, although Ashton Gate station was brought into temporary use from 1970 to 1977 for 'soccer specials' and again in 1984 when the American evangelist, Billy Graham, preached to a vast crowd at Ashton Gate Stadium:

I'm an absolute train fanatic and have no real recollection of using it. I've used it twice on train specials since they've re-opened it, but cannot recall using it as a lad. I can remember always wanting to be tall enough to see over one of the road bridges down the far side of Greville Smyth Park. There were some black wooden railings that you could see through but obviously an adult could see over but I couldn't. I always wanted to see the trains. I've always been interested in trains and going to sleep at night in Clift Road, you could hear the shunting going on in the goods yard [Ashton Meadows sidings] which was absolutely massive and I believe at one time was one of the biggest in the south west. To me, [this was] rather a comforting sound but I don't know why. (Stephen Williamson)

The line has been replaced by a new, single track laid, reopening in 2002 and now used solely by freight trains which serve Royal Portbury Dock.
As well as being provided for by a nearby station, people in this part of Bristol also lived close to the pleasure steamers which operated from Hotwells, taking trippers both up and down the River Avon and on out into the Severn and the seaside resorts on the north Somerset coast. Dorothy Pike describes such trips:

I used to go up to Beeses Tea Gardens, that was quite nice. Of course Campbell's pleasure steamers used to come in quite frequently to Hotwells. They used to go down

Janet Steel believes this informal snap was taken on the Mendips near Cheddar, in the late 1920s-early 1930s. Left to right are Janet Steel's grandparents Mr and Mrs William and Mary Amesbury, their next door neighbour Kathleen Gillard of 13 Frayne Road, and Janet's father William Harold Amesbury.

Eddie Beaven's aunt and uncle – his mother's sister Bertha Stubbs (née Parkhouse) and Edwin Stubbs (Ted to everyone).

The picture was taken about 1948 alongside Bertha's brother's caravan at Uphill, Weston. Eddie's father recalled getting water from a stand pipe and milk in a jug from the local farmer who owned the field.

as far as Ilfracombe. It was six and sixpence [which] was quite a lot of money then! You used to catch it down Hotwells, under the suspension bridge. The Rownham Ferry was there. When they built the new bridge they took the ferry away. I don't think it was used much, not really, but it was always there and on the low tide, you walked across. Of course, [you] went across in the boat in the high tide. And there was the Gas Ferry as well, and the Rownham Ferry, no Mardyke Ferry. Mardyke is still going isn't it, but I don't think the next one is, the Gas one's gone isn't it?

The seaside was a popular destination for family holidays in the late 1940s and 1950s. The Hickery family used to go to West Bay in Dorset 'for a couple of weeks'. John recalls Mr Farley, who owned a garage on Coronation Road, driving them there. Around the same period, Lew Pedler's family 'spent about two or three years on the trot' in a caravan at Brean Down, lent to them by the owner of Bacon and Sons, Furniture Removers:

Mrs Bacon and her husband had a caravan at Brean and they used to let it out to customers. Basically we were offered the caravan. It was a homemade caravan, very comfortable, but you see a lot of these guys who had trades or their own businesses would make their own caravans.

Local adventures
The Ashton Court estate, in decline from the end of the Second World War when it was used by the army, and finally taken over by Bristol City Council in 1959, provided the perfect spot for curious local children to explore, as Lew Pedler explains:

The other place we used to break into was Ashton Court which in those days was still owned by the Smyth Family and you had to climb the walls to get in. The house itself was fairly redundant, the old lady [Esme Smyth] had died by that time anyway. In one of our mad moments, we charged over the wall along Beggar Bush Lane, a lot of bushes around there. In we got and the next thing we knew we were actually being confronted by the army who were using the place as a training ground and had fixed bayonets coming towards us! You've never seen us shift so fast. Must have been half a dozen of us. We shot over the wall, but we didn't shoot over the wall where we'd come in. We just shot over the wall and realised in mid-air we weren't hitting ground when we'd expected to. That frightened us. We used to go over there fishing 'cos there were a few ponds over there, but we were unofficial guests.

Lew visited the mansion house, this time as part of a legitimate group:

I can remember at school being part of an organised party that went over Ashton Court when the building was beginning to get in a serious state of disrepair. The army had moved out, the orangery was collapsed inwards but we were allowed to walk around the rooms. One of the teachers from Southville [Secondary School] had arranged for us to go and look around it. I can remember one of the lads, Barry Moore, who is still around, wrote a story. It was a local education [authority] competition and he won it on his story about a description of what he called 'The Magic Library'. There was one of these clever little catches on one of these façade library books which opened out into a tunnel and it apparently got King Charles off the hook when he was doing his charge through, because the Smyth family were royalists I think, so he was protected.

Later still, Lew learnt the fate of Ashton Court mansion itself from a work colleague:

I worked at Merrywood School in 1961 [or] thereabouts. The caretaker Bill Henderson had formerly been a glazier with the city engineers and one of his first jobs was to go over to Ashton Court and actually re-glaze and secure the building and he said the whole place had been gutted out inside. A lot of the stuff which we see today was destroyed by the local authority when they moved in – anyway, either it had collapsed and nobody had any sort of vision then to try and bring it back into any sort of order again, whereas these days you'd restore it.

John Hickery also paid covert visits to the estate:

We used to go out Ashton Court, climb over the wall. The only danger we got in out there was we were out where the golf course is in bushes and there was army people there training. Suddenly they came running at us. We seen them come and dived behind the bushes. They were poking the bushes with bayonets and they never seen us. They weren't really concentrating. My sister was with me then as well, my younger sister.

As a boy, Roland Reed recalls visiting Ashton Court estate on a day when it was opened to the public as a special event:

I remember going up to Lady Smyth's. It was open to the public and I remember going over for conkers and the gamekeeper locking us in and we had to go over to the top lodge to get him to let us out.

In the days when it was considered safe for children to stray further from the family home, Leigh Woods provided an ideal haunt for local children in search of adventure. When asked if he had ever played in Leigh Woods as a child, John Hickery gave an emphatic reply, as well as a clear description of the great rock slabs on the western side of the Avon Gorge which were used as slides:

Oh yeah – good God, all the time! Donkey Slider. That's the donkey slider the first one, you know the one I mean? Eat Less Bread – the steepest one, 'cos after the war, things was short and they got up there and they painted Eat Less Bread all the way down and that's what it was always known as. That was in the second valley. The first valley was where the Donkey Slider was, the second valley is still there but I don't think the writing's there. We used to call this one the donkey slider 'cos in those days, you'd go over there as kids [and] that was just like a sheet of ice it really was. We was up and down to the top where the [railway] tunnel goes under there, get on there and you'd shoot down. That was brilliant! Eat Less Bread was more a great big thing it was, and it only had one gulley you could slide down. But oh – we used to go along there all the way to Pill. That's a dump innit! You never forget Pill.

Christmas celebrations

Events at Christmas time also feature strongly in people's memories. Peggy Triggle, recalling the days when trams ran along Ashton Road, describes the special tram which was laid on by Bristol Tramways Company just before Christmas:

> When the trams were in – this is before the war – it was lovely at Christmas time to see a tram, all done up in the lovely Christmassy lights and things, and it would come right down here, and we'd go down and see it. That was such an exciting moment for us! We were thrilled, weren't we, to go down and see that tram going down, all lit up at Christmas time.

Once trams had disappeared from Bristol's streets, a special bus toured parts of the city at Christmas, as Barbara Hickery describes:

> It was a big bus for the Lord Mayor's charity and just before Christmas it used to start off up, I think, in Clifton and make its way through town. [It] used to be all lit up and Father Christmas used to be on there. That was the highlight of Christmas that was. Of course it used to come up North Street and I'm trying to think where it ended up. I think it went up to Bedminster Down. [Arranged by the] *Evening Post*, [it] might have been. I know it was to do with the Lord Mayor 'cos we used to get the Lord Mayor's parcel at Christmas. They used to give out 'cos our mum was on her own and I remember her saying that was lovely.

Alma and Bernard Chalmers remember taking part in the annual round of carol singing in the nearby streets, organised by Ashton Gate Methodist Church:

> We loaded an organ, a hand-held organ, on to a truck and we used to trundle it along from Ashton Gate Methodist Church to sing carols and one of the main stops was Farley's garage. We always sang carols there and were given mince pies from the big house. As I remember, it always seemed to be a wet or foggy, smoggy night when we did this.
>
> Mr Farley was connected with Ashton Gate [Methodist] Church so that's why we

always went there and we were always given a warm welcome. Another place we always went was Frayne Road because there were connections there from the church as well and we always had more mince pies and a cup of tea. We'd pick the ones where we knew we'd get a welcome! (Alma Chalmers)

Bernard began his National Service in 1950 and pinpoints the carol singing trips taking place in the late 1940s:

It's either then, or when I came back [from the army]. It must have been rather earlier than later as old Mr Farley was still alive. Now these were nights when you had all the smogs because of the coal fires. And every Christmas, they used to go out with this hand thing singing carols. It's on a little trolley, right, which you'd pull along. It's not a hand organ. You'd push these pedals with your feet. So the trolley's got the organ on it and a seat for the chap who's going to play it. He don't stay on it while you pull it along or else it will be too heavy. So he pushed the organ and played the keyboard. And you'd come out the Chapel and you'd start to work your way up – Ashton Gate Road is it? – and the first house you'd stop at is number six 'cos that's Mr Symons who goes to the Chapel; and you'd work your way along to the end of there – you'd turn right and you'd come out into the top end of Walter Street. And then you'd go up Walter Street and you'd go down – which is now the back of the Centre 21 old folks' home. It wasn't that then – it was houses. And you'd turn right and there's a road that runs out to the Coronation Road. In that road there's another elderly lady who goes to the Chapel, so we'd stop there and we'd sing some more carols you see. Then you'd go down Coronation Road towards the park and you'd go in which is now a car lot and then you'd turn right and you'd come up against a Victorian house which is where Mr Farley lives – old Mr Farley – and you'd play some more carols and he lets you in and you'd have mince pies. That's your last trip for the night. You were going to church members, but we're singing it out in the road, so anybody else can see. It also reinforces their position locally as members of our church you see.

Special events
Some events really stand out in people's memories. Eleanor Roosevelt, widow of President Theodore Roosevelt, visited Bristol in the early 1950s

9 Frayne Road (c1908). Typical of the 33 houses which form the terrace overlooking Greville Smyth Park. Note the original sash windows and the balcony with its serpentine supports.

A detail from the tilework in the vestibule of a Frayne Road house.

A typical cornice from a house in Frayne Road. Most of the houses have only one room with such a display, but the room and the style vary.

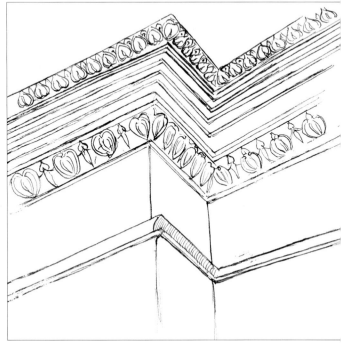

as part of her world tour to champion the Universal Declaration of Human Rights of which she was a leading author. Dorothy Pike was one of a number of local people who met her:

> Oh yes, I shook hands with her. She came to a meeting over at the church, that's right. Over at the school. Ever so nice, an elegant lady. Yes, she shook hands very kindly. At St Francis. I always belonged to St Francis. Well it was a women's meeting at the school. We used to hold a little meeting on a Tuesday afternoon. She was visiting the towns and looking at the destruction, and she came over there to our meeting that particular afternoon, and shook hands with us, all the way round. I remember I had one of the children on my arm. A very nice lady. A big woman she was, rather.

The Coronation of Queen Elizabeth II in June 1953 was a great opportunity for people to get together and celebrate. One of Lew Pedler's aunts, who lived in Brislington, owned a television set – a rarity in those days – and family and friends gathered at her house to watch the Coronation take place:

> I can remember crowding round this ten-inch thing and because I was [one of the] younger elements, you parked your bum on the floor and the adults sat on chairs and you had this completely crowded room – and a pretty small room! I look at it today and think did we actually get all that number of people in this room. If there was a street party, I wasn't involved in it. I remember being in the last year at Ashton Gate School, so we were ten or eleven then. I can remember we had the Coronation magazine, in fact I've probably still got it somewhere, a Coronation book that every school kid was given. We had a mug and we also had a Coronation souvenir booklet so that you could follow the service as it went through. Every Friday afternoon was project so any subject of your choice well of course we were all into the Coronation because there was plenty of newspapers, wasn't there, for cut-outs for your scrapbooks and whatever else. We had to write about how it all came about [and] I can remember doing mine and always being criticised – 'Oh, you copied that'.

Twenty five years later, people had a further excuse for a Royal celebration, this time to mark the Queen's Silver Jubilee. Stephen Williamson describes the events which took place in Clift Road where he had grown up and where his parents and aunt still lived:

I can remember a very nice street party in 1977 for the Queen's Jubilee – 25 years on the throne. We were married by then but went back for the street party. We sort of gatecrashed the Clift Road one. There were still a lot of people I knew there and Dad was out with his bottles of wine, handing them out and keeping everybody well topped up. The road was closed, tables down the middle of the road yes. I can't recall sitting down and eating – probably more buffet style – but there were tables down the middle of the road. It was very … in and out of people's houses, not just walking in and out but I think we had Martin [eldest son] who was only six month's old I think we spent a reasonable amount of time in Mum's. I'm sure somebody had music but I couldn't say [for certain] they had big speakers blaring out. It was certainly an enjoyable occasion.

Chapter 9

ASHTON GATE – THEN AND NOW

We always used to go to each other's and have a cup of tea. You didn't have coffee much in those days like. You used to go in and have a cup of tea.

Sheila Hall

As well as recounting specific incidents in the lives of ordinary people, this book is about change. In recalling childhood friends, neighbours and family life in times past; when remembering where particular shops once stood, the goods they sold and the characters who ran them; in describing the games they played as children and the excitement of picnics and outings by train, the people whose stories are at the heart of this book have described a life that has moved forward.

The process of change is, in the main, a subtle affair: the disappearance of familiar landmarks and regular haunts – such as a favourite shop – is, perhaps, its clearest manifestation. Photographs of Ashton Gate taken in the first part of the twentieth century show just how well people in the area were provided for by shops and we have a number of first-hand accounts of buying food in the immediate neighbourhood, as well as being provided for by visiting tradesmen. Apart from a number of 'corner shops' which have long since disappeared, both North Street and Ashton Road boasted a wide variety of shops which catered more than adequately for the everyday needs of the local residents. Smaller shops selling items of food, such as traditional general stores, bakers and greengrocers, have nearly all gone, largely driven to closure by the coming of supermarkets. Where the demand for a particular product persists, the supply continues, the best example being places to eat and drink. Our research shows that in 2009 there are more bars and cafés in the immediate area than in 1950, in a few cases occupying the same premises but under different management, but far fewer other shops.

The Second World War brought change to the area in a less subtle manner. Compared with the major destruction of the historic heart of Bristol, the docks and large parts of Bedminster, Ashton Gate suffered less serious damage from wartime bombing. In spite of this, we have clear evidence from people who lived here throughout the blitz of the severe upheaval and hardship imposed by the war – of families such as the Pikes, whose house and possessions were completely destroyed and the Amesburys, who decided to leave Bristol altogether for a safer life elsewhere. The comradeship which developed whilst sheltering in the neighbours' Anderson shelter or under the nearby 'bonded warehouse' did little to dispel the sense of fear. Similarly, the stories we have recorded of the fun and games which children enjoyed on local bomb sites, mask the reality of sudden destruction and the changes which it brought to this part of the city.

Over the years, a few once-familiar buildings in this part of Bristol have disappeared. The Clift House, standing on land now occupied by Riverside Garden Centre, lives on in name only: Clift House Road and Clift House Spur. Brenda Hatter can recall remains of this imposing building which was demolished sometime in the 1930s:

> I can still remember certain walls with greenery up around it and I know as you went in the entrance, and my parents' allotment was on the left. All I can remember is there were like arches as though it was perhaps basements, but it was all very old and just the brickwork would have been there. So it [Clift House] must have been there then.

More information about the Clift House can be found in Chapter 10.

Newcomers to the area will have no idea that until very recently the Ashton skyline was dominated by the giant Wills Factory No.3 which ran along much of the length of Raleigh Road and whose picture featured on some brands of WD and HO Wills cigarettes. At a more human level, post-war 'slum clearance' saw the wholesale removal of several streets of terraced houses such as Walter Street, confirmed by Alma Chalmers who grew up there. Wartime bomb damage was generally made good, such as St Francis's Church on North Street, attended by a number of people in our stories, which was rebuilt in the 1950s.

Another example of physical change in this corner of Bristol is the alteration to the local road system over the years in order to cope with the growth in motor traffic. Prior to this, trams operated to and from the city centre along Ashton Road to the terminus on Ashton Avenue Bridge, as Dorothy Pike recalls:

That was the end and then it would turn round and come back. It had an arm and a wire and it used to rattle down through, and of course it was ever so frequent, you could rely on one every few minutes, very, very frequent indeed. I had to go to town [by tram] to work. Of course trams had an open air upper deck and slatted wooden seats that you put backwards and forwards if they were wet.

The parade of shops in Ashton Road, with the Rising Sun (now Bar BS3) on the extreme right and the Cooper's Arms on the left. The tram is on its way to the terminus at the end of Greville Smyth Park. Taken in 1938, the railings are yet to be removed for the impending war effort. (Courtesy of Memories Photos, Bristol)

Long after the last trams ran in this part of Bristol, the first major changes to the local road system were made in the 1960s, prior to the closure of the Ashton Swing Bridge. Brenda Hatter describes what happened:

> Well originally [the whole of] Coronation Road was two-way and I suppose at one time Clift Road was two-way, Clift House Road was two way then they decided to alter it around. You came down Coronation Road and you went straight down towards the park. Then they decided to change it and they made Clift Road one way. Then they decided they'd make Frayne Road one way and Clift House Road. They altered it from going up to coming down and my mum visited me one day and walked across the road and was knocked down by a car because she was looking the wrong way. It was chaotic!

Once the Cumberland Basin flyover was complete in 1968, further alterations were needed and Lew Pedler explains how traffic was re-routed:

> As far as I can remember, when you had the new bridge built in Cumberland Basin, all the traffic flowed along Clift House Road and I think Clift House Road was one way. When it got to the junction of Coronation Road it split; it either went down towards Ashton Road, so you either went to Long Ashton Road or left to North Street, but at the junction of Coronation Road, the other road normally turned up into Coronation Road, Clift Road was one way up, not sure what happened to Frayne Road. Then when they completed the Ashton Avenue Scheme to join up with it all, that's when they turned the traffic round the other way because they didn't allow any traffic to go up over into Ashton Road direct, you had to go round the loop to get to it.

Mervyn Southway, who lived in a house on Clift House Road from 1950 until 2006, described the road prior to all the changes as 'a very, very nice, quiet road. There was little traffic went through there.' He also recalls the proposal to create a large roundabout where Clift House Road met Coronation Road, and the implication for residents in the immediate locality:

Cars were a rarer sight than now, but nevertheless here are five proud owners.

Stephen Williamson attempting some minor repairs on his Ford Anglia 422 EON, which he owned from 1970-74. His Dad's Ford Cortina Mark 3 is parked in front of his car, and Lionel Butt's Austin Cambridge, he thinks, is opposite. Being able to park in Clift Road around 1972 was clearly much easier than at present!

Anthony Gingell outside his home 32 Frayne Road in March 1967. Anthony was a salesman for Frost and Reed, and this was a company car.

Sheila Hall in front of her wedding car in 1959. The Ford car, which was green and cream, is parked outside the door to the living space beside and over Tommy Rowe's shop, 300 Coronation Road.

Tommy Rowe with his car in Clift House Road.

Karen Thomas, Anthony's brother, with her Grandad Austin Gingell, and her dog called Boo outside 32 Frayne Road in 1962. This was Karen's first car, a Morris 8 Series E. Note how the car is pointing in the opposite direction to the current one-way route.

Well all I know is, they were knocking down the houses because they were going to build a roundabout. Now I don't know what that would have done, I'm sure. That was all of our houses in Clift House Road, the ones down Coronation Road to Clift Road, and the ones on that side of Clift Road – all that lot was coming down!

This scheme as a whole was eventually dropped, but some demolition was carried out in order to widen the roads at this point. Tommy Rowe's corner shop at the junction of Clift House Road and Coronation Road was a casualty, and his daughter, Sheila, who was living above the shop at the time, recalls what happened when the Council declared its intention to demolish the property:

It was for the road widening. They had a petition and a meeting and everything to try and stop it, but they couldn't. There wasn't anywhere to stop, to go in the shop either you know. For buses used to come up and down here as well, you know in those days. And they had it for the road widening and he tried to stop it happening but they always win in the end.

According to Lew Pedler, 'I think the Corporation made him [Tommy Rowe] an offer he couldn't refuse'.

By the time the new road system was in place, Tommy Rowe had gone to live in a house in Bedminster Down and Sheila Rowe married and moved into a house on the opposite side of Coronation Road from where her father's shop had stood. She describes one particular incident involving a confused motorist:

My husband and I were stood by the gate and we were watching the traffic go round and round and then this car stopped and said, 'Please can you tell me how to get out of here cos I've been round four times!' Yes, 'cos it was one way look, instead of having two ways – and as I said, he kept on going round and round and didn't know how to get off. Yeah. And he swore 'cos he was a bit angry at having to keep going round and round!

The new road system was regarded as something of a challenge by a few local motorists. Riding his motorbike, John Hickery 'used to cut down that way against the flow. I got stopped one day by the police and the neighbours were out there, cheering! "What are you doing?" [the police asked] "Well I live here!"'

For some, the building of the fly-over system meant new places to explore and spaces in which to play, although Mervyn Southway confirms that 'a big portion' of Greville Smyth Park was lost when the fly-over was built:

> Yes I remember the building of [the flyover] as a 16 or 17-year-old. I used to love kicking a football around and that flyover, just inside the park, I used to go down and kick a ball for hours up and down the concrete slopes because it nearly always came back to you. I also used to take my mum's dog out at the same time so the dog would have a run and I would have a play. (Stephen Williamson)

How have the inhabitants of Ashton Gate responded to change? None of the people interviewed complain that life today is any worse than it was in times gone by, although several speak with great fondness of the happy times they had as children, growing up here. Play routines have altered over the years and we have a number of accounts of how playing in the street outside one's house was the norm for many children in the age before mass car ownership. Greville Smyth Park has always been a popular venue, but as the number of cars increased from the 1960s onwards, the option of using the street as a safe play space gradually disappeared and children were forced to use the nearby park, as well as going further afield for adventure. This was at a time when parents had fewer concerns than they do today about the risk from strangers and children were allowed to roam further from home. With many forms of 'play' now computer-based, recent research indicates that children in the early years of the twenty-first century spend increasing amounts of time either at home or in their friends' houses.

The disappearance of local employment opportunities enjoyed on the scale which existed when the nearby Wills factory and supporting industries were in full production is likely to have impacted adversely on the sense of community in the area, but we have unearthed little or no evidence of this.

Two winter shots taken three years apart from the balcony of 32 Frayne Road. The left-hand picture in full snow in1963 shows the edge of C bond warehouse, and Clift House Road on its original course winding towards its passage over the top of the Ashton Swing Bridge. Three years later, in the winter of 1966, the trees and road have gone as the Cumberland Basin flyover scheme is completed. Clift House Road is one way, causing some confusion, as our writers have said!

This earlier photograph shows the final section of road in the Cumberland Basin scheme, leading to the new bridge across the Avon, but with the bridge itself incomplete. Note the swimming pool in the park, bottom right, mentioned by our contributors. (Courtesy of Bristol Record Office)

Work on the road scheme is now finished, but the old Clift House Road route to the Ashton Swing Bridge is still visible. With the upper road deck of the bridge removed soon afterwards, the redundant railway deck beneath has become a popular pedestrian and cyclist route across the river. (Courtesy of Bristol Record Office)

In the street

Amy Gingell, Karen's mother, outside her home, 32 Frayne Road in 1968. The car is Karen's Austin Cambridge, her uncle Fred's old car. Fred was running the Rising Sun public house in Ashton Road with his wife Kitty Wyatt.

12 Frayne Road in the 1920s, the home of Janet Steel's parents and grandparents until about 1953. As with the picture of Clift Road below, the front windows have venetian blinds as well as curtains.

1 Clift Road, Mary and Lionel Butt's home, taken in the 1930s. Note the venetian blinds in all of the windows, and the impressive climbing hedge.

Amy Gingell admiring her blooms at her home 32 Frayne Road, in 1968.

5 Clift House Road. The picture is undated but must have been taken around 1908, as shown by an uncompleted adjacent house on the original negative. Pictured are Francis Short and his wife Eliza, with their daughter-in-law Nellie [seated] and her daughter Marcia. Mr & Mrs Short were the grandparents of Thelma Short, who supplied the earliest personal photograph in this book.

Frayne Road. The appearance of those in the picture suggests it was taken early on in the street's history, but after 1919, as C bond warehouse is already built. Some local talk of the small girl with the pram being Dorothy Pike was soon quashed when she calculated that she would have been eight in 1919. The identity of these early posers remains unknown! (Courtesy of Memories Photos, Bristol)

The bottom of Frayne Road about forty years later. This time we know who took the picture – Karen Thomas's visiting Danish pen-friend – but we don't know the identity of the young boy fascinated by the road-mending equipment, nor the road-menders.

Karen Thomas's mum, Amy Gingell, walking home in Frayne Road. Taken in August 1961 by Karen's pen-friend visiting from Denmark.

What of the landmarks that remain in this corner of Bristol? The southernmost of the three distinctive red brick 'bonded warehouses' continues to dominate the immediate landscape, clearly visible from miles away. The Toll House on the junction of North Street and Coronation Road may have changed use over the years, currently housing people with mental health problems, but may still be easily recognised as the same building depicted in early photographs. Similarly the tannery on Clift House Road continues to operate a production system which has largely remained unchanged since Victorian times in buildings which have seen little or no changes. Houses in the area may have been altered and modernised over the years and the overall area the subject of a certain amount of gentrification, but in most cases, mainly externally, still retain the architectural features typical of the age in which they were built – the opening years of the twentieth century.

Wedlocks on Ashton Road has been a victim of pub closures and was demolished in 2009. However, the Coopers' Arms, also on Ashton Road and recently given a coat of paint, is a thriving 'local', providing a reminder that the Ashton Gate Sunrise Brewery once operated just a short distance away. The Rising Sun, although now known by a different name after major refurbishment in 2008, is also a popular meeting place. Karen Thomas remembers the pub at a busy period in its history when it was run by her aunt and uncle. As well as visiting her cousins there, Karen used to help out from time to time, such as football match days:

> It is a big pub, it's got function rooms upstairs, its living and function rooms. We all sort of went to help out. And weddings – we used to make the sandwiches and what have you.

Like countless similar communities both in Bristol and other large cities, Ashton Gate may have changed physically over the years, but the strong sense of community and togetherness remain. Shortly before she died in January 2008 aged 97, Dorothy Pike summed up her feelings about living here nearly all her life:

> It's always been a nice area – nice camaraderie.

Chapter 10

CLIFT HOUSE AND ITS ESTATE

The Clift House, or Redclift House, has left little mark on the landscape apart from the road names Clift House Road and Clift Road. However, people in our stories remember the ruins of the house before it was completely demolished, and this chapter uncovers some of the facts and legends about the house and its surrounding area.

When it was built (and the date is yet to be discovered), Clift House stood in its own grounds and estate. Close to the house on the west was Colliters Brook, which now runs beneath Greville Smyth Park, with the estate running eastwards from the house and bound on the north by the New Cut. A photograph[1] taken in about 1890 (see p161) from Rownham Hill shows a fine house set in mature woodland overlooking the Suspension Bridge and the Cumberland Basin. However, maps show that by then the estate to the east of the house had been developed into the industries which are still recognisable today. It may be that its proximity to the river and docks has meant that Clift House is now better known locally for what has been built in its grounds than for the house itself. Hence this account starts by describing those industries that developed alongside the New Cut in the grounds of the old house, before piecing together what we know of the dwelling.

Clift House estate industries

Travelling eastwards from the entrance to Clift House there were three adjacent manufacturers – the tannery, the iron-works and a shipyard.[2] These were served originally by the river and then by the New Cut and Coronation

Road as it turned out of Bristol towards the Ashton Turnpike toll-gate. Also on late-nineteenth-century maps is a 'nursery', between the tannery and Clift House. By this time the House was owned by Bristol Corporation and the nursery was used 'for growing plants which in summer adorn the open spaces of the city'.[3] The site was still in use in 1923, known as William Hill's Nursery.

The tannery was and still is known as the Clift House Tannery; a nineteenth-century occupant of Clift House, Mr Thomas Ware, gave it its current trading name of Thomas Ware & Sons. The tannery also had two small dwellings attached, the doors of which can still be seen where Clift House Road joins Coronation Road. Around the latter half of the nineteenth century these Clift House Tannery cottages were variously occupied by an accountant, a tannery engineer, a currier and the tannery foreman, and their families.

Adjacent and to the east of the tannery was the Hemmings Iron-works, famous for supplying corrugated iron pre-fabricated buildings to the colonies. The works occupied 10 acres 'in the grounds of Clift House', and local newspaper accounts and advertisements in the 1850s described how the visitor could see 'streets of shops' in situ before they were dismantled and

CLIFT-HOUSE IRON BUILDING WORKS, NEAR BRISTOL.

An etching of the Hemmings Ashton Gate site, showing the prefabricated buildings before being dismantled and shipped off to the Colonies. This picture was published with an article describing the Hemmings Works in the February 15th 1854 edition of the *Illustrated London News*. The article and others around the same time are fulsome with praise and wonderment as to the ingenuity and diversity of the buildings constructed here, and we are left wondering if the illustration uses any artistic licence in portraying how all this fitted into a space behind and around the current tannery! (Courtesy of Bristol Record Office) shipped overseas. The *New York Times*[4] correspondent was impressed with how 'the erections are entirely put together with iron screws and bolts and may be put up by any inexperienced person in a few hours'. The cost of a two-roomed cottage in 1852 was £50, but a 'cheaper sort is made for £35'. The Bishop of Melbourne had ordered a church with 600 sittings for £1000. The Hemmings Iron-works remained there until about 1854–5, when the business consolidated in London.

Next to the iron-works was the third industrial enterprise, the Vauxhall shipyard, with its slipway down to the New Cut. The slipway is visible in aerial photographs and is still evident through the gates of the current works,

An aerial shot of the New Cut, the Docks and the Clift House estate, stretching across the foreground. Probably dated 1945, a part of Clift House is visible on the far left behind the warehouse.

A closer aerial view of the east (Bristol) end of the estate, taken from the same shot. The Vauxhall shipyard's slipway can be seen running into the river, and also a house at the far right, on the Coronation Road. This is likely to be the house of the shipyard owners, the Payne family. (Courtesy of Bristol Record Office)

which are in-between the tannery and the modern Vauxhall House and petrol station. The Red Clift Yard, where James Martin Hillhouse is known to have built warships and other craft between 1780–86, pre-dates the building of the New Cut and would thus have been on the bend of the River Avon. The site was apparently later occupied as Bedminster Yard by Messrs Acraman, Morgan and Co. for a short period from 1840–44. Mr Acraman, a City councillor, spoke eloquently, if not impartially, in a debate in 1840 on 'The Docks Question', saying that he was not only a councillor but a rate payer and that he 'had purchased Clift House and its grounds…. for the purpose of manufacturing large iron and other steamers.' Acraman's businesses were varied, including tea importing (their company co-owned Bush House, now housing the Arnolfini) and 'iron and tin plate merchants, and manufacturers of chain cables and anchors.'[5] Later still the premises were known as Vauxhall Shipyard, owned by John Payne. In 1881 the widowed Emma Payne was living on the premises. The shipyard closed in 1925, although in 1939 there was still a maritime connection directly opposite in Coronation Road – a 'boats fitting company', proprietor E. Payne.

The outbuildings

Maps and the census show not only Clift House but stables and a lodge. In fact there were at one point two lodges. One was at the beginning of the carriageway to the house, opposite the toll-house in Coronation Road. The tree-lined carriageway ran approximately in line with the alley now running between Frayne and Clift Roads. The other lodge was at the entrance to the walled estate, located under the current warehouse. Census returns from 1851 onwards show that the outbuildings (sometimes known as Clift House Lodge and Clift House Cottage) were usually occupied by one or more gardeners and their families, though by 1881 Clift Cottage was rented out, and in 1891 the Clift House Lodge was occupied by a park ranger, presumably of the adjacent new 'Bedminster Park'.

A quiet corner of Somerset?

Although this book is dedicated to the living memories of the twentieth century, the area in earlier periods was busier and more thriving than we might imagine. What is now Clift House Road turned into a public footpath leading (across a bridge over Colliters Brook) to Rownham Ferry; to the south-west of the estate were Fraynes Colliery, more iron-works (now Brabys) and a route to the South Liberty Lane coal-pits. The construction of the railways brought more people to live and work nearby.

Perhaps then it was no coincidence that between 1800 and 1900 the Clift House, its occupants and its industries are regularly reported upon in the *Bristol Mercury*. The articles describing incidents of theft and violent attacks, business developments and, latterly, protests from local residents are a reminder that this small corner of Bristol was not as isolated as we may believe before Ashton Gate was developed for housing. Indeed the House in its earlier days could have benefited from a Neighbourhood Watch, as it was burgled a number of times, all the subject of thorough police investigation and justice.

The *Bristol Mercury* published accounts of these burglaries and trials. One account relates how, on December 1st 1824, Lady Smyth's home was broken open by 'a strong lever applied to the bottom of the window frame.' The villains opened all the doors 'more securely to effect their retreat' and set about purloining plates, knives and garments. A week later it was reported that six men and a woman had been apprehended. When on trial at Somerset Assizes some four months later, more of the story and their detection came out. Apparently two of those charged were seen the next day 'with mud on their clothes – of a peculiar sort – country-mud.' Seen going from pub to pub in search of warmth on a snowy night, a suspicious witness informed Lady Smyth's butler, Mr Plumley. They were charged with the theft of 'three silver spoons, a black cloth shawl, a black silk coat, a grey pelisse, and a table cloth.' The jury consulted a short time and returned the verdict of guilty. They were sentenced to death. About 160 years later, an Australian correspondent to the *Bristol Evening Post* identified her great-great-grandfather as being one of the culprits, confirming that he had in fact been transported, not hanged.

In May 1838[6] there was another scandalous occurrence – theft and a near-fatal stabbing of a policeman trying to apprehend a thief. The 'ruffians' were brought to justice when a policeman on duty at the 'turnpike gate on Ashton Road' got a lead from 'a rough looking Gloucestershire man working as an excavator on the Bristol Exeter line.' As before, the villains were arrested in a pub.

A final extract from the *Mercury* describes how Mr Hemmings was threatened by '200 men, some with picks and shovels, for alleged late payment of wages to a railway sub-contractor.' Fortunately for him he was able to send a message to the police station and the crowd was dispersed. Hemmings was not only the occupant of the House and the owner of the iron-works in its grounds but also a contractor for the construction of the nearby Exeter railway. An advertisement in the *Mercury* in 1838 seeks 300–400 men for stone-breaking, as well as a nursery able to supply large numbers of tree 'whips', presumably for planting alongside the line.

The house and its occupants

The author of a 1914 *Bristol Observer* historical sketch of the House was unable to find early records until a mention in 1799 of land tax paid on 'a tenement known as the Red Clift House in the parish of Bedminster.' The owner was one George Bush, who lived at 'Redclift, near Wapping', so it may be that that was the origin of the house name, rather than there being another Redcliffe in Bristol. The Bristol Docks Act of 1803 mentions the cutting of a new course (the New Cut) from a 'certain place called the Redcliff into the present course' of the Avon. A map illustrating the Jessop's docks redevelopment plan shows a house named Redclift on the southern shore of the proposed new course of the Avon, bounded on the south west by Colliters Brook.

Redclift House then passed into the possession of a Lady Nill, from whom it was purchased by the Smyths of Ashton Court in 1800. It became the Dower House for Dame Elizabeth, the widow of Sir John Hugh Smyth, when he died in 1802. In 1814 Dame Elizabeth took out a 'bond of indemnity' against the property for £1000 from the Dean and Chapter of Bristol Cathedral, who were clearly not averse to lending money.

It is perhaps significant that on April 23rd 1822 the Dame took part in the opening procession to celebrate the new turnpike road 'known as Coronation Road', along the course of the New Cut. This brought the property and its grounds within easy reach of road as well as river transport, and the industries

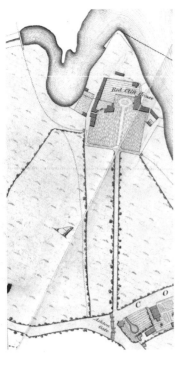

A detail from the 1828 Ashmead map of Bristol, showing Redclift House with its carriageway running from the toll road behind the Ashton Gate. Top left is Colliters Brook running via an unamed 'pill' or inlet into the Avon. The alleyway behind the houses on Frayne Road and Clift Road more or less align with the route of the carriageway.

of tanning, ship building and the Iron-works became all the more economically attractive to develop in the vicinity.

The dowager died at Redclift House in March 1825, and the next known occupants are a Mr Daniel Stanton who died in 1834[7] and then Mr Hemming in 1840. A year later the House's demise started, with a lease to a Bristol firm granted by Sir John Smyth. The firm went bankrupt and the mortgage held by the bank was called in. The bank sold the house to John Proctor in 1850, although the 1851 census shows the house as 'uninhabited' neither by owner nor staff. Proctor apparently sold it on to Stephen Cox in 1868, although Cox had in fact already been in occupation of the house and the tannery since 1854. His tannery business, Cox Bros,[8] had started in Nailsea but their main yard became that in Bedminster. In 1861 Stephen Cox was described as a 'Tanner employing 68 men', and he lived in Clift House with his wife Martha, their five children and four live-in servants. Ten years later the whole family were still there, and one of the same servants, Lydia Taylor.

Mr Cox, a councillor for Bedminster, was apparently annoyed at the public being able to walk across his 'fine carriageway' as they traversed the intersecting footpath from Coronation Road to Rownham Fields. He persuaded the council that it would be a great improvement if the path were to be in a tunnel beneath the carriageway; however it is not known if this work was undertaken. Cox retired in 1877 and in 1878 the Bedminster tannery yard was taken over by Thomas Ware. Thomas Ware occupied Clift House as a tenant until he died in 1890.

A photograph[1] taken around 1890 from Rownham Hill looking towards Ashton Gate. In the foreground is the New Inn (near the present police stables), and in the middle the lock entrance to the City Docks. In the background, with woodland around and behind, is Clift House. Note the retaining riverside wall of the estate, and to the right of this a tidal inlet which is the mouth of Colliters Brook. (Courtesy of Bristol Record Office)

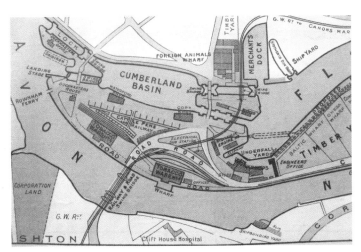

An extract from a plan of Bristol Docks, dated May 1908. Clift House is described as a hospital. Note bottom right the [Vauxhall] shipyard and its slipway, and also the footpath running from Coronation Road to the river Avon to the old Vauxhall Ferry. The ferry had by then been replaced by the current Vauxhall Footbridge just downstream to the right [not shown in this picture]. (Courtesy of Bristol Record Office)

In August 1876 Bristol Town Council purchased the house and about seven acres of land for £6,000. From this point onwards the property seems destined to have attracted industry not just in its backyard but on its very foundations. The purchase was in order to create a sewage works on the site, but apparently this 'excited the opposition' of the occupants of Clifton to such an extent that it was scrapped. The House remained occupied, being home in 1891 to one Thomas B[r?]own and his two children, a widowed and retired British general. Another watery intention in 1899, to turn the site into a pumping station, was so controversial that a city-wide poll rejected the proposal by a 2-3 majority. Never short of a controversial scheme to put in someone's backyard, the Health Authority had already in 1893 proposed that the house be turned into an isolation hospital for 'fever cases'. Ham Green estate was purchased in that year for the same purpose. Ashton Gate residents met to protest at a public meeting in 'the Iron Room' (this may have been in the Iron Chapel, which was on the site of what is now St Francis Church). The chairman Mr H Harvey contended that 'there was no particular reason to single out West Bedminster' and perspicaciously noted that 'things originally intended to be temporary became permanent.' The audience rejoindered with 'hear, hear', and the report continues, 'the winds would carry the infection from this fever spot over Clifton – and he hoped they would enjoy it' [laughter]. Other speakers said it would be dangerous to those using the [Rownham] ferry and that the 'contiguity of a hospital for infectious diseases to a people's park would be extremely undesirable.' As ever, a further speaker was concerned about the effect on 'surrounding valuable properties.' Mr Latham wound up the proceedings with a populist approach, reminding those present that 'two thirds of the population in the neighbourhood were working people whose health and strength were their capital.'

The campaign was not successful though, as the house became a fever and diphtheria hospital until 1906. After this ceased the stables were apparently still used for ambulances. Clift House's final lease of life was in 1914 as a temporary reception for people being treated for tuberculosis. Perhaps fittingly, as a pioneer in seeking a cure for TB a hundred years previously had been Thomas Beddoes, working just across the river in Dowry Square.

An undated photo showing Clift House, foreground centre, with C Bond warehouse in its garden. To the left of the house are allotments, adjacent to the river and the swing-bridge. (Courtesy of the M. Tozer collection)

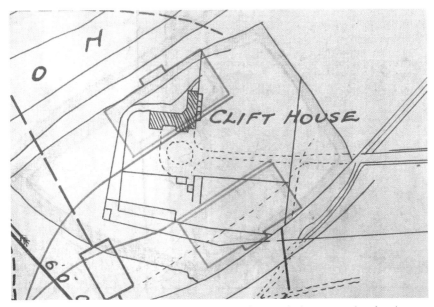

1912 Docks Engineer's drawing of the house and grounds in preparation for the two planned warehouses (only one of which was built), showing sewerage and water mains and the rectangular outline of the warehouses. Also shown is the main carriageway to Clift House, which started opposite the toll-house in Coronation Road. (Courtesy of Bristol Record Office)

A photograph captioned 'D Company, 14th Gloucesters leaving Bristol', presumably during or just before the First World War. At the rear along Clift House Road are the trees at the entrance to Clift House. The warehouse is yet to be built, but there appear to be three scaffolding towers. The sign hanging over the pavement, reading 'W Hill', is that of the nursery. Along the road are tannery buildings that have since been replaced by the semi-detatched 'Dutch houses' nos 8 and 9 Clift House Road. These were owned by the tannery and occupied by staff, as described in one of our stories. (Courtesy of Bristol Record Office)

The ending

Clift House's disappearance behind the 10-storey C Bond Warehouse in 1919 was the last chapter in its history before subsequent demolition. In 1899 the *Bristol Mercury* speculated as to its next use 'or indeed whether its chequered career is not ended by the Harbour Railway extension works.' By the time a potted history was published in the *Bristol Observer* in 1914[9] it was indeed ready for its last few years.

The 1914 article intimated that the house would soon be demolished 'in order to provide a site for one or more of the giant tobacco warehouses.' In fact only one was built (the plans[10] on p163 show another proposed warehouse alongside the river), and Clift House remained standing long enough for an aerial photograph (estimated to have been taken in the 1920s)[11] to show it dwarfed in the shadow of C-bond warehouse. Now, visitors to the Riverside Garden Centre beside the warehouse can spot an elegant Scots pine that would have been in the grounds, and staff speak of a stone retaining wall and terracing along the river bank. There is even talk of recent building works having revealed a cavern that may have been the House's cellars. However the most lasting memorial is probably the naming of the extension of the once quiet Clift House Road as part of the 1960s Cumberland Basin development – officially called the Clift House Spur.

Endnotes

[1] Bristol Record Office Item: 40353/34a

[2] It is not always clear in the accounts as to the boundaries of these various works, and further research is required

[3] *Bristol Mercury* October 13th 1899

[4] *New York Times* July 26 1853

[5] *Bristol Mercury* February 8th 1840
From rate books: http://www.lookingatbuildings.org.uk/cities/bristol/bush-house/dating-bush-house.html

[6] *Bristol Mercury* May 12th 1838

[7] *Bristol Mercury* January 1834

[8] Nailsea and district local history society pub.: *The Nailsea tannery*

[9] *Bristol Observer* May 16th 1914 E.T. Morgan 'Clift House and its history'

[10] Bristol Record Office Item: Docksplan/arranged/75

[11] MJ Tozer collection

Sources

The Times archives
    Dec 11th 1828
    May 14th 1838
Bristol Gazette – transcribed in Bristol Record Office item 41648/P1/51
    Dec 9th, 16th & 23rd 1824
    April 7th 1825
Bristol Observer May 16th 1914 E.T. Morgan 'Clift House and its history'
Bristol Mercury – on-line archives courtesy of Bristol City Council Library services
Bristol Censuses 1851–1891 (Bedminster ward)
Malago Magazine no:25 for interpretation of the aerial photo showing Clift House and also the denouement of the 'silver spoons' theft story

Acknowledgements to

Roy Webber in *Bristol Industrial Archaeology Society Journal* no: 18 1985 (p5 ff) particularly for information on the shipyards.

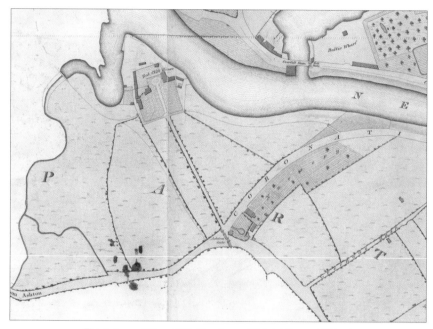

The Ashmead Map 1828 (Courtesy of Bristol Record Office)

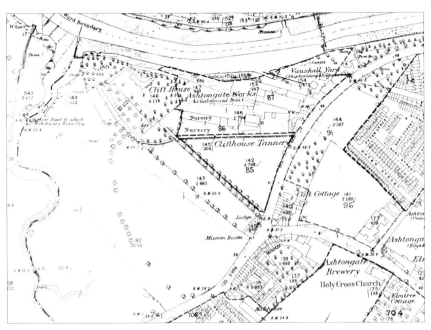

1865 (Courtesy of Ordnance Survey)

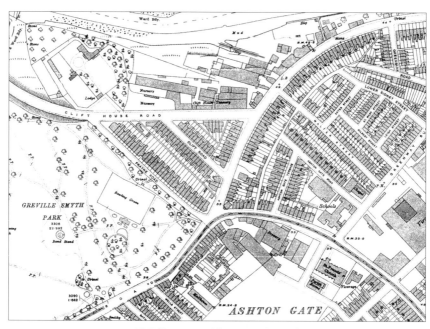

1918 (Courtesy of Ordnance Survey)

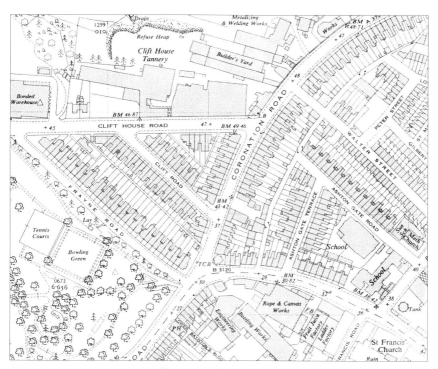

1951 (Courtesy of Ordnance Survey)

INDEX

Further copies of this book can be obtained from
John Holland, 19 Frayne Road, Bristol BS3 1RU

email: smallcornerofbristol@googlemail.com